LOVED BEIN'

by

Ron Modell

COPYRIGHT

Loved Bein' Hear With You Copyright © 2014 by Ron Modell

MoLo Publishing
9224 Karlov Ave
Skokie, IL 60076
www.molopublishing.com

The views expressed in this work are solely those of the author and do not necessarily reflect the views of the publisher, and the publisher hereby disclaims any responsibility for them.

ISBN: 978-0-9890520-2-3

MoLo Publishing Date: 7/01/2014

DEDICATION

Dedicated to my beautiful wife Kathy,
and my dear brothers Sandy and Lance

ACKNOWLEDGEMENTS

For many years my beautiful wife, Kathy, had strongly encouraged me to write an autobiography of what she thought was "an incredible life." Her constant plea was that my vast range of life experiences should be recorded as a history for my family and friends, and that many others would want to enjoy it also. Thank you, my love, for persisting.

To my publisher and graphic designer, Mark Ohlsen, friend, ex-student, colleague (during the national stage band camps), and most of all, "adopted" son for over 40 years, your excitement, expertise, and enthusiasm in seeing this project go forward, gave me the momentum to keep writing until it was done. My sincere thanks.

As my dear friend and recognized author, Michael Hirsh told me, "It's very hard to write a book!" How right he was. To Mike, and the many people who helped put this together, Rebecca Partiff, Rick Calderon, my daughter, Lisa Marie (for the many hours of transcribing until I discovered the Dragon program on the computer), and my cousin Lili Davidson, a very special thanks. I am deeply indebted to my dear friend, Sari Max Fiss, and my cousin Emil Davidson. But the most important person who truly made this book possible, was my incredible editor, Laura Iandola. Working with her on this project was not only a learning experience, but a real joy.

Photo Credits:

Barry Stark—Northern Illinois University Media Services, Kathy Modell, Vern Spevak, Bonnie Modell, Bob Kornegay, "Captain" Todd, Hotree/Charters, NOVUS, Al Stewart, Christina Severson

Cover Photo by David Gross.

Cover Design: Mark Ohlsen and David Gross

CONTENTS

REVIEWS

"Not only is this book informative and hilarious, it outlines enough wonderful experiences to last five lifetimes! Ron Modell is a gifted storyteller and musician and one of the greatest college jazz band directors ever to have taught."
Bravo my friend,

Vincent Di Martino
Professor Emeritus, Centre College
Danville, KY

"Ron Modell's memoir is loaded with rich details about his fascinating life. He makes all the characters that he's encountered--from grade-school friends to world-renowned pop stars--into relatable humans, treating every story with grace and humor. It offered new insight into a guy I've called "dad" since I could talk."

Josh Modell
GM/Editor-in-Chief, The A.V. Club
The Onion

"Ron Modell, a world-class trumpeter/educator, invites the reader into his personal life-time travels to meet other musicians who with him have made history in their lives of jazz, symphony, and pop music. His true stories of bringing entertainment and education to multitudes of participants and listeners world-wide cover both a serious yet very humorous life. *Loved Bein' Here with You* intrigues the reader's emotions to join Ron's very personal anecdotes in this *can't stop reading it* book."

Richard H. Cox, MD, PhD, DMin
Adj. Professor, Duke University Medical School
Scholar, Georgetown University Center for Clinical BioEthics
Artist/educator, Conn-Selmer, Inc.

When I met the Mode in 1979, he self-identified as a music educator and I inferred that he'd played professional trumpet since his *bris*. But I also saw he was so much more than that--he just didn't know it. Fact is, I don't believe Ron discovered himself until he wrote *Loved Bein' Here With You*. Do yourself a favor and read it. You'll connect with his journey and laugh your ass off in the process.

Michael Hirsh, author-journalist and producer-director of
"One Year in the Life of the Greatest College Jazz Band in America"

FOREWORD by Quincy Jones

In 1996 The Montreux Jazz Festiveal celebrated "50 Years of Quincy Jones Music." The Festival Director, Claude Nobs, had retained the Northern Illinois University Jazz Ensemble to be the band that would back all the great artists appearing at the event. People like Patti Austin, Toots Thielemans, and Phil Collins for starters. I was first introduced to the band's leader, Ron Modell, at the first rehearsal. Although I'd just met him, as soon as I heard his band play, I knew a whole lot about him.

The band knocked me out. They performed at the highest level. This was a college band? Their professionalism. musicianship, togetherness, and joy at making music together jumped off the bandstand. Their enthusiasm was infectious. They were exciting. And they could swing.

That kind of passion, dedication, discipline, and unity of purpose doesn't just happen by itself. It is the result of many, many hours of hard work, practicing alone and together, and singular focus. It requires a tremendous commitment of time. Making the many sound like one – is no little accomplishment. And it always comes from the top – from the leader. He or she sets the tone and creates the atmosphere that permits the band to grow together. The band is a reflection of that leader. He's the motivator, the motor. And the unquestionable motor of this band is Ron Modell -- the "Mode" to band members.

But Ron Modell is way more than just a bandleader, he is also the man who created the Northern Illinois University's first jazz program in 1969 and built it from the ground up. He shaped and molded the program, spending countless hours promoting everything from Student compositions and arrangements to concert bookings. Then he added to his Human Dynamo creds by publicizing the program, recruiting high school students for the Ensemble, and appearing anywhere and everywhere from other schools to prisons. And the NIU Jazz Ensemble was creating lots of excitement and pride among the student body. Lots of folks noticed. In 1983 Downbeat named them the top college band in the country. Long before that recognition, NIU understood that engaging Ron was one of the best decisions the university ever made. When they committed to building a jazz program at their school he is the man they turned to. Talk about a lucky choice! From the start Ron attracted major artists like Dizzy Gillespie, James Moody, Clark Terry, and Louie Bellson to tour with the band, hanging out with the student-players, glad to answer their questions and pass on any wisdom they had to offer. And later, gigs were noticeably upgraded. The ensemble started appearing at venues like Chicago's famous Jazz Showcase and The Chicago Jazz Festival where they played before 30,000 people. Add to that a couple of European tours where they scored big with audiences wherever they went.

NIU is also fortunate that Ron happens to be an outstanding trumpet player – the man has serious chops – and a superlative musician. You want versatility? Before becoming a full-time educator, Ron was First Chair in two symphony orchestras, played the Borscht Belt, backed Tony Bennett and Mel Torme, and gigged regularly with Machito.

Despite such a varied, impressive background, I'm sure Ron's proudest accomplishment would be his commitment to work as an Educator. He didn't just teach his students about music, he passed along life lessons that would benefit them all in whatever they did for a living. He made them understand that a teacher – that person up there trying to prepare them for a successful life – was really their friend. And in the process, everyone was able to have a good time.

Really, the book is a love story. It's about the love of music, but also of people in general. Ron just naturally generates so much positive energy and good will that people just can't help giving it back. And his notorious sense of humor – humor a la Mode -- was an asset in his dealings with everyone. He just makes people around him feel better. And that enthusiasm, that love, that energy bounces back and forth between him and the musicians – and among the musicians, too. You can hear it in the music.

I have nothing but admiration and affection for Ron who will always be a valued friend, but that's not why I recommend this book...

It's just a great read. A fun read. But don't let all the humor make you lose sight of the fact that there's a lot of serious, valuable information here. A lot of wisdom.

There's also no doubt that you'll laugh a lot. Guaranteed!

Q.

PROLOGUE

Whether it was playing lead trumpet for the legendary Tony Bennett, or doing a duet with the great opera singer Joan Sutherland at her American debut with the Dallas Civic Opera, conducting the Northern Illinois University Jazz Ensemble on the main stage of the Montreux Jazz Festival in Switzerland, putting together a big band for pop star Phil Collins to do a two-month world tour, or lecturing to Motorola Corporation's top 115 world executives on motivation, I feel as if, when added up, my opportunities and experiences could not possibly have fit into one *lifetime*--but they have!

I am almost eighty years old. I have been married four times, have six children, and have moved from New York City to Tulsa Oklahoma, to Dallas, Texas and finally to DeKalb, Illinois where I have resided for the past 45 years.. I've had four angioplasty procedures, and yet with all of that, I can tell you with absolute certainty that the single most difficult day of my life was July 4, 2007, at 9:10 pm in Dekalb's Hopkins Park. I had just performed as soloist for the thirty-eighth consecutive year with the DeKalb Municipal Band. Now, as I exited the stage, I came face to face with the decision I had made: I would never play the trumpet again. And I never have.

I began playing the trumpet when I was seven years old, had my first professional paying gig when I was fourteen, and landed my first steady job, playing at a resort hotel in the Catskill mountains of New York, at the age of fifteen. My two uncles, Milton and Louis Davidson, were highly regarded professional trumpet players, whom I loved, respected, and tried to emulate for my entire career. In 1953, while touring with the actress Cornelia Otis Skinner, within a six-week period, I auditioned for renowned conductors, Eugene Ormandy, Leopold Stokowski, and George Szell. For an eighteen-year-old with no more experience than playing in the Bronx Symphony Orchestra, I now fully understood the great Yiddish word "chutzpah" (unabashed nerve).

So on July 4, 2007, as I put my trumpet in its case for the last time, the cold hard fact was right there: what will my life be without the trumpet?

This memoir is the story of my life with the trumpet and without the trumpet. It's the story about discovering not only my love for making music, but also of teaching it to young people while preparing them for life's trials and tribulations. I was most fortunate to end up at Northern Illinois University in DeKalb, Illinois, where I was able to create a nationally and internationally acclaimed jazz ensemble. The result of having found my calling early on, coupled with an intense commitment to the life of a musician and educator, meant that for 65 years I was able to get up each morning eager to go to work.

As you journey through my life, in which humor has been ever present, you will come to understand that my final career came as naturally as playing the trumpet or teaching. At the age of seventy-two, I performed my first standup comedy routine at McCurdy's Comedy Theater in Sarasota, Florida. Having the ability to make an audience forget all of their troubles while you are on stage feels as wonderful to me as any performance I ever remember on the trumpet.

Spending eighteen summers in the Catskills exposed me to America's greatest Jewish comedians, whom I've always drawn on for inspiration. The first joke I ever delivered onstage at McCurdy's was about an elderly Jewish woman on the TV quiz show, "The $64,000 Question." On national television, the show's MC, Hal March, asked her, "Mrs. Goldberg, for $64,000 who was the first man?" Mrs. Goldberg replied (in a demure manner with a Jewish accent), "For a million dollars, I wouldn't tell you that!"

BROUGHT UP IN THE BRONX

For the first two-and-half-years of life, I did not utter one word. Not even an "aah," "goo," or "dah." All my parents heard was a moan or a groan, or they saw my finger pointing at different objects. My mother was really starting to panic. They took me for hearing tests, but the results were normal. I was not yet ready to speak.

It finally happened in May of 1937, when my parents were driving from our apartment in the Bronx to Bensonhurst, Brooklyn to visit my father's parents. As we came off the Brooklyn Bridge and sat waiting for a red light to change, I noticed on my right—and I remember all of this vividly—the brightly-lit marquee of the Brooklyn Paramount Theater. At this point, the light changed, and as my father attempted to go, a very sweet-looking dog passed in front of our car. It stopped, and as Pop tried to maneuver around this poor frightened animal, it kept following the path of the car. All of a sudden, a small voice from the back of the car said, "Will someone tell that son-of-a-bitchin' dog to get out of the way!"

My father drove right up onto the sidewalk! Fortunately, nothing was hit. The front door on my mother's side flung open, and both my parents turned to my older brother Sandy and demanded, "Did you say that, Sandy?" "No, Ronnie said it," he replied.

How's that for an opening line? They made me repeat it, and when we arrived at my grandparents in Brooklyn, they had me say it again. We jumped back in the car and drove all the way back to the Bronx so I could repeat it for my mother's parents.

I can see now that what I felt then about getting a rise out of people by saying something funny has continued throughout my entire life. As I approach my eightieth year, enjoying my latest career as a stand-up comedian, I see how much laughter can do for your health, both body and soul.

All four of my grandparents were immigrants. My father's parents, Rebecca and Charles Modell, were born in Poland. I know very little about them, as we only got to see them once a year at Passover. A the Passover service, when my grandfather Charlie went through the entire Seder, my older brother Sandy and I would crawl around beneath the dining room table. I can't think of another time in our lives when we were more bored. First of all, we were starving, and if you know the service you really don't get to eat for a long time. My mother also thoroughly disliked her mother-in-law and made Sandy and I quite aware of her feelings.

Anna and David Davidson, my mother's parents, came from a little *shtetel* (a small village of poor Jewish people), called Bialastok. Some of the time the Russians ruled; sometimes it was the Poles. I remember as a young boy hearing that my grandfather David immigrated to American in the early 1900s, and had to work several years before he could afford to send for my grandmother Anna to America. My grandfather was a wall-paperer and house painter. He also played the clarinet and was part of a group of Klezmer musicians in Europe.

My mother Gertrude, their first child, was born in 1908. She had two brothers: Louis, born in 1912, and Milton, born in 1919. At the age of 10, after studying piano for a year, the teacher told my grandfather that Uncle Louis was not showing any real promise. Grandpa consulted with his friends at their social club, and though I have no idea of how the trumpet was selected, the next order of business was to find a really good trumpet teacher. The number one trumpet teacher at that time was Max Schlossberg, second trumpet in the New York Philharmonic. He charged the royal sum of two dollars a lesson, and Uncle Louie began studying with him at the age of ten. Amazingly, by the time he was fourteen, young Louis was playing in a salon orchestra aboard the USS Leviathan, a ship that sailed from New York to Europe and back.

Louie went on to become one of the greatest symphonic trumpeters of his time. At sixteen, he was given a contract to play in the Cincinnati Symphony under Fritz Reiner. After five seasons in Cincinnati he moved back to New York, and in 1935, he was engaged as principal trumpet of the Cleveland Orchestra under Artur Rodzinski, and later George Szell. In 1939, Maestro Arturo Toscanini invited him to be his principal trumpet on a tour of South America. Louie's final years were spent at Indiana University's School of Music, where he distinguished himself as one of our country's finest teachers.

Max Schlossberg was my uncle Milty's teacher as well. My grandfather David told me Schlossberg had said to him, "Milty is the greatest pure talent I have ever heard play the trumpet." But he added, "If I was Milty's father, I would beat him with a stick to make him practice." While Louie would faithfully practice three to four hours every day, Milty would come home from school, drop his books, grab his baseball glove, and run out to play with his friends. Often my mother would lie for him when her father invariably asked, "How long did Milty practice today?" Louie chose to stay strictly in the classical field, but Milty would become a more versatile trumpeter. In addition to serving as principal trumpet for the Ballet Russe de Monte Carlo, the Dallas Symphony Orchestra, and the New Jersey Symphony, he also became one of the busiest club date trumpeters in the New York-New Jersey area. I have not met many people in my lifetime who would immediately light up a room when they entered. Milty was one of them.

When either Milty or Louie would visit my grandparents' home, you would have thought that royalty was about to grace their apartment. Uncle Louie had an incredible taste for what we called "New York Bialys" (similar to bagels), and there had to be at least a dozen of them on the table when he arrived and four dozen packed carefully for the trip back to Cleveland. All of the wonderful dishes that I would give anything to taste again were prepared and presented: gefilte fish, chopped liver, stuffed cabbage with a raisin filled sweet and sour sauce. And those were just the appetizers! Along with music and comedy, food was always important throughout my life.

My mother told me that as an infant I was a real crier, but at 5:30 every afternoon when a New York radio station would start their broadcast with trumpeter Clyde McCoy's theme "Sugar Blues," I would become completely silent. I think it was preordained that the trumpet would become an important part of my life!

My first memory of actually hearing a live trumpet was when my uncles would visit my mother's parents in the East Bronx. When I was seven and my brother Sandy was ten, Uncle Milty set up a meeting with one of the best trumpet teachers in New York City, Bert Pennino. Hard as he tried, he could not get Sandy to make a sound on the trumpet. Me, being the typical seven-year-old, kept asking let me try, let me try. I think probably to shut me up, Bert handed me the trumpet, and I played immediately. At that point Bert looked at my mother, pointed to Sandy, and said, "Don't teach *him*, teach him."

Three years later I had my first trumpet lesson with Jimmy Smith, the third assistant first in the New York Philharmonic. I could not have studied with a more kind and gentle man. Jimmy taught me from the Edwin Franko Goldman book, popular for beginning students, and after a year or so I was sent to study with Sol Lubalin, then fourth trumpet in the New York Philharmonic. He immediately got me into the trumpeter's bible, the Arban's book. We worked together for about a year.

I then moved on to another great teacher, Joe Rescigno, who had played with the Metropolitan Opera from 1919 to 1949. Joe lived in Flushing, Long Island, and I had to take several buses to get there for my Saturday morning lessons. To once again have a sweet, gentle, and kind man as a teacher was a real blessing. When I first met Joe, he had a hearing aid in his breast pocket that looked like a portable radio. We studied exclusively from a book called *Rhythmical Articulation*, by Pasquale Bona. In preparing me for a career as a symphonic trumpeter, almost everything I played for Joe had to be transposed into the keys of A or C, and sometimes D. This course of study was like basic training: scales, rhythmic drills, and transposition. The only real piece of music I ever got to study with him was a Rossini solo, "Inflammatus." Joe had a son, Nicola, a famous opera conductor, who would become an important person in my musical life twenty years later as my conductor in the Dallas Civic Opera.

Joe also had a grandson, Joseph Jr., who became famous in the opera world as a phenom. I saw a demonstration one day at my lesson, when a prominent singer from the Metropolitan Opera was visiting. In his teaching studio, Joe had a hundred or more librettos stacked on a shelf probably six feet high. What I saw that day was a three-year-old boy told to go find the score for *La Boheme*. Joe Jr. climbed on a ladder, selected a book, went to the piano, and began to play the first notes of the opera. They tested him on several more operas, and he played them all flawlessly.

When I was twelve years old, my uncle Milty took me to the Bach factory to pick out a trumpet mouthpiece. I had just received my first trumpet. At the factory in Mount Vernon, a man laid out a black velour cloth and laid thirty or forty mouthpieces on it. Milty said to pick up each one, put it to my lips, and see how they felt. After I don't know how many mouthpieces, I settled on a 7B, and I played that mouthpiece for twenty years.

Murray Karpilovsky was my next teacher, and there is no doubt in my mind that he was the game changer. My first three teachers had laid the foundation and prepared me to make the next big step. At 6 foot 4 and 240 pounds, Murray was the most powerful trumpet player I ever heard. His demeanor in teaching a lesson was quite different from what I had experienced with my other teachers. He was extremely demanding and had me studying out of the most difficult books I had ever encountered.

I was about sixteen when I started to work with Murray and was already a pretty cocky young man. Things reached the boiling point when I came for a lesson on which I had labored for many hours, and after playing it, I thought perfectly, Murray's response was "That was completely wrong." Try to imagine this young high school trumpet player, taking his trumpet and almost shoving it into the hands of one of the greatest players in the country, and saying, "Here, you play it for me!" Murray played the entire etude louder than I have ever heard a trumpet played in my life, after which he told me, "Pack up your trumpet and go home; I'm not teaching you anymore." I took two buses back to the Bronx, and as soon as I saw my mother I broke into tears. I was smart enough to realize just what I had lost. It took two weeks, along with phone calls from my uncle Milty, my mother, and my grandfather Davidson to finally get Murray to relent and accept me back as a student. At my next lesson, before we played one note, he said to me, "For the rest of your life, let your actions speak louder than your words."

While my uncles' influence on me was certainly profound, we are now going to get into a very special subject—my mother, Gertrude Davidson Modell. Little Gertie was short, probably five feet tall, but she was a powerhouse, a dynamo, the typical Jewish mother of that time.

To truly describe her would probably take me years of psycho-analysis. Although she could be hysterically funny, more important were the things she did as a mother to nurture the kindness and sympathy that Sandy and I,along with our younger brother Lance, developed about helping other people. As young boys, Mom taught us to always help the older people in our building. Our five-story building had no elevators, so anytime we saw an older neighbor walking with groceries, it was our duty to immediately take their bags right out of their hands and escort them up into their apartment.

Before the advent of supermarkets, Sandy and I were sent to shop at the neighborhood stores. There was a shop for everything, from bakeries to fruit-and-vegetable stands to "appetizer stores." I remember how Mom would send me to the fruit-and-vegetable store and tell me, "Now you go there and you ask for Sam. You don't go to anybody else but Sam. You tell Sam that you are Mrs. Modell's son and that you want two tomatoes. Because Sam knows the kind of tomatoes I want and how to pick them for me." It was that way in almost every store. Where today lox can sell for $40 a pound, Mom would tell me, "Go get me ten cents worth of lox" and they would cut off one or two slices. It was a wonderful time, when I think back on it. It was a marvelous time. One of my mother's favorite jokes was about a little Jewish woman who went at nine in the morning to the fruit-and-vegetable stand and asked the vendor, "Can I have two pounds of onions?" The man replied, "Madame, we don't have any onions right now, but we expect a shipment at noon and if you come back then, I will be happy to give them to you." She walked out but returned an hour later and asked the same clerk, "Mister, can I have two pounds of onions?" The guy said, "Lady, I just told you an hour ago, we don't have onions but are expecting a big shipment at noon. Come back then, and I will give you all the onions you want." She came back an hour later, and of course it was only 11 o'clock, and once again asked for her two pounds of onions. By this time, the guy was really ticked off, and he asked her, "Madame, can you spell?" She replied, "Certainly I can spell!" And he said, "Well, take the word 'bullet' and leave off the last three letters, and what have you got?" And she said, "Bul." "Right," said the clerk; "Now take the word 'letter' and leave out the last three letters, and what have you got?" "Let." "Now take the f-u-c-k out of onions and what have you got?" She told him, "There ain't no fuck in onions." "That's what I have been trying to tell you!

My little brother Lance was a very picky eater when he was young. One day we went to an all-vegetarian restaurant on Southern Boulevard, just Mom and Lance and I. The Jewish waiters had a bad reputation in most restaurants—they were all very mean because they didn't want to be working there. My mother told our waiter, "Please bring this little boy a vegetarian cutlet, and make sure that you bring him mashed potatoes and peas, because he is a very fussy eater and doesn't like anything else." The waiter brought Lance a plate with a vegetarian cutlet, French fries, and string beans, and when my mother asked about the mistake, the guy said in a nasty voice, "I forgot! You want my head? Take my head! I forgot!" At the end of the meal—my mother always carried a pad and pencil in her purse—she wrote him a little note: "Dear waiter, I forgot your tip. Take my head!" That was Gertie.

It was also typical Gertie when I visited my folks in Oakland, New Jersey, where they had moved from the Bronx into their winterized summer bungalow. I suggested a movie and took them to see "Coming Home," with Jane Fonda and Jon Voight, about a paraplegic who falls in love with a nurse. So here we are, sitting in this darkened theater together, watching the movie, Gertie between my father and me. All of a sudden the movie turned sexual, and because Voight's character was paraplegic, they began to have oral sex. Well, as soon as he went down on her and she went down on him, in this little movie theater, out of a clear blue sky comes this very loud voice, "This is what you bring a mother to see? This filth?" My father and I both ducked down under our seats, so all you saw sitting there was one woman. It was perfectly timed and incredibly funny. By the way, she didn't leave until the end of the movie.

My mother had a tremendous influence on her three sons, not all of it positive; I am sorry to say. Both she and her mother could be described with the Yiddish word *farbissener*, which means an embittered person. Their husbands never did enough, never earned enough, never got them into places they felt they should have been. I remember at the funeral of my wonderful father Nathan; his friend John came up to me and said how much he would miss my father. I wasn't trying to be funny, but the words just came out of my mouth: "You know, John, I never met any person who didn't love and adore my father, except two women—his wife and his mother-in-law." It really was the truth. Pop had incredible qualities of kindness and gentleness, and to this day I miss him terribly.

Although Gertie and Nat were married for fifty-four years, I have no recollection of seeing any physical affection between the two of them. There was an occasional peck on the cheek, or a hug good-bye, but nothing like the intense feeling that I have for my wife Kathy. Here's another example of Gertie being Gertie. In her later years, she became ill and was admitted to a hospital, some thirty minutes from their home, before being released two weeks later. You will not believe the story I'm about to tell you, unless you knew Gertie.

For fourteen days my dad, who was seventy-five years old at the time, would get up in the morning, have his breakfast, and then make the half-hour drive to the hospital. He would stay with my mother until after lunch, drive the thirty minutes back home for a bite to eat and a quick nap, and then return to the hospital, at my mother's side until visiting hours were over in the evening. He did that for fourteen days! While she was in the hospital, I spoke to my mother every few days. If I didn't, I was sure to hear, "Did you forget you have a mother?" On one of my phone calls, I innocently commented, "I'll bet you've received a lot of get-well cards." "I have received many cards," she replied, "but you'll never guess the one person who didn't send me one: your FATHER!" Does that give you some idea of what my dad had to put up with for fifty-four years?

I must acknowledge that during the last years of their marriage they really did become close and take care of each other. Gertie's last weeks were spent in a nursing home in Oakland, New Jersey. There was a nurse taking care of her, and my father would tip her quite handsomely to give my mother special care. Pop told me that just three weeks before Gertie's passing she had given the nurse ten dollars to disappear while my father visited so she could "service her husband." That was Gertie!

It must certainly be acknowledged that my mother raised good sons, and I was blessed to have two wonderful brothers. Sandy was three years ahead of me, so as children we never had a close relationship. My memories of our early years include playing games together, fighting with each other and going to the Star Theater on Southern Boulevard in the East Bronx every Saturday morning, where we would enjoy three movies and a serial. After the movies, we'd stop by a delicatessen and order corned beef sandwiches, french fries, and cream soda playing a round of the old odds-and-evens finger game to determine who would have first pick of the french fries.

The two of us were very different: Sandy was a serious, straight-A student, while I was the kid whose mouth never saw a stop sign. Mrs. Kaufman, who was the fourth-grade teacher to us both, told my mother bluntly, "If you paid me a million dollars, I would never believe that you are the mother of both of these boys."

We separated when I left in 1952, going on the road at the age of seventeen with Cornelia Otis Skinner and then moving on to Tulsa, Oklahoma from 1953-57. Sandy, meanwhile, went on to receive his degree from City College of New York in 1955, and then on to service as an Ensign for two years in the U.S. Navy.

Our younger brother Lance, born ten years after me in 1944, was the baby of the family, adored by all, and always the center of attention. At a very early age, Sandy and I would play cards with him—gin rummy, or a Hungarian game called klabiash—and Lance was a terrific card player. At that time, our mother was working part-time for an attorney and not at home in the afternoon, so Sandy and I would take care of Lance. It was a thrill.

Lance had a wicked sense of humor, as you can see in this story when he was around ten years old, and I was home visiting my parents. Lance had pleaded with me to take him to a famous ice cream parlor called Jahn's, on Fordham Road. He HAD to have a hot-fudge sundae on this hot, steamy June day, and he kept bugging me until I finally gave in.

I drove up to Jahn's and, of course, there was no place to park, so I told Lance, "Look. I will double-park here, run in, get your sundae, and we'll take it home to eat." Now, if you double-park in New York City, you can get a big, fat ticket. When I came back with the sundae, not only was there a police car right behind my car, but the windows had fogged up inside and Lance had written on the back windshield, "HELP! I am being kidnapped!!" I got in that car as fast as I could and drove off. That was Lance.

The affection and love that Sandy, Lance, and I felt for each other grew deeper with the passing of time, always enriched by the wonderful memories we shared as children. Those memories are even better because of the presence of my father, Nathan Modell. I have to say that even though I was fortunate to meet and work with many great people over the course of my life, my dad was my number one guy. "Pop," as we called him, worked for most of his life as a New York taxicab driver on the night shift in the vicinity of Times Square. My brothers and I didn't get to see him much, because he would arrive home from his shift as we were getting ready to leave for school, and by the time we got back from school, my dad would be getting ready to go to work. We always cherished the time we had with this very kind and gentle man. Others did as well: the Broadway actor Louis Calhern would ride with my dad and ask him to pull over, keeping the meter running just so he could talk to "Pop" in conversations that lasted an hour or more. To my surprise and delight, I found him to be an even more profound person as he got older.

Growing up in the Bronx near my immigrant grandparents meant we were constantly exposed to "old world" thinking and ways. After my first child, Scott, was born in Dallas, I brought him to visit the family in New York six months later. When I took Scott to meet Grandma and

Grandpa Davidson, my grandmother opened the door but refused to let me come in, hollering to her husband to bring her a piece of sugar. Both of them, by the way, spoke very little English and conversed almost entirely in Yiddish. My grandfather finally brought a piece of cube sugar, and after breaking off a tiny piece and putting it on her pinky, my grandmother rubbed it inside Scott's mouth.

After we were invited in, and I put Scott on the bed, I asked what had been going on. My grandmother explained that Scott had never been in her home before and that from now on every visit should be as sweet as the first. At this point, I noticed Scott peering in the mirror of her vanity, and I went over to turn him around so he couldn't see the mirror. Startled, my grandmother asked me why I had done that, and I told her my mother had told me a baby should never look in a mirror before they had their first tooth. My grandmother's response was to look at me hard and say, "Oh, your mother and her silly superstitions!"

Beginning in the summer of 1941 when I was seven years old, my parents and grandparents rented a New Jersey bungalow to escape New York City's oppressive heat and humidity. Our little colony of West Oakland contained some fifty Jewish families that returned summer after summer. For me, those two months were like being in paradise, waking up early in the morning, heading out to the apple tree near our bungalow, and meeting the guys who became like brothers to me.

We were truly the boys of summer. After breakfast, we played a game or two of softball. If it was really hot, we headed for the Ramapo River to jump in and cool down. Back home for lunch, and then a game of mah-jong. Can you believe that we all became really good mah-jong players? Or we might play pinochle, gin rummy, poker, or board games

When I got a bit older, I organized the younger kids into a baseball team, the West Oakland Raiders, and we played other teams from around the area. It was enormous fun to work them out every day, and it gave me great satisfaction to give them some discipline and the experience of playing together. I am in touch with some of the West Oakland Raiders, in particular Donny Perlman, who is very near and dear to me still..

The summer of 1948 would be the last year of being with that old gang of mine. I was recruited to be a junior counselor at a local day camp across the river, a place where I had brought our baseball team to play. At the age of thirteen-and-a-half, I was assigned, along with a senior counselor, to take charge of twenty-seven six- and seven-year old boys. Spending each day that summer with these wonderful kids was a kind of farewell to my childhood, and I cherish the memory.

Every day after lunch I would take all of the boys to a quiet place to sit under an enormous oak tree. There I would improvised an ongoing story, a kind of Bronx Scheherazade, that would leave the boys eager to hear the next day's adventure. The highlight of our summer together was our planned expedition to the top of the mountain across the Ramapo Rvier, an event I wove into my stories as we sat in the grass in full view of the mountain. The story sparked their imaginations, for I had solemnly told them that there was a real possibility of encountering some American Indians still living on the mountain.

Every afternoon as they boarded their bus for home, the boys would all look intently at me, wondering if tomorrow would be the day we would climb that mountain. Each day I responded to them with a very serious face and merely shook my head, "No." All summer long, I nodded "No." Finally, one August afternoon, keeping my grave demeanor, I nodded "Yes," and the boys were elated.

The next morning twenty-four of twenty-seven boys showed up with cap pistols strapped to their sides while the remaining three were armed with pop-rifles. We could have traveled by bus for our trek, but I made it even more dramatic by using a rowboat to take them, two at a time, across the river. As we started to hike up the mountain, we reached a point where I could look down a ridge. Unknown to the boys, I had hidden a feathered arrow in my pants, which I snuck out, flipped up in the air, and which landed perfectly upright in the ground, in front of us. Instantly twenty-four pistols flew out of their holsters, and three shotguns loaded and ready to go as all twenty-seven boys hit the ground. Three of them were so scared they began to whimper, "I want my mommy." I assured them there was no reason to be afraid, and that I would go ahead and speak with the Indians. Walking to the top of the ridge, I summoned up my memories of all the old cowboy-and-indian movies I had seen and affected what I thought sounded like an Indian dialect, delivered in a loud, firm voice: "Chuckalaka mumba!" I pretended to listen carefully for the Indians' reply, then turned to the boys and gave them the "come ahead" sign.

What a way to end an incredible summer. The love and affection the kids and I felt for each other is one of my best memories. Where are you now, Steve Spector?

P.S. 48/JAMES MONROE HIGH SCHOOL: GETTING TO KNOW THE PRINCIPALS

I attended Public School 48 in the Bronx from K through 8. My schoolmates were often in trouble, or in gangs, although it pales next to what we see today. In those days, if you merely smoked a cigarette you were considered a bum. My eighth grade class had sixty-six students, and I later learned that twenty-two of them would eventually have some kind of criminal record. One was even electrocuted for murder. But in many ways it was your typical Bronx neighborhood, a mixture of Italians, Jews, and Poles, with some African-Americans. I remember most of the tough guys tended to be Italian.

On the fifth floor of PS 48 was a bulletin board that actually announced the day's fights. Every day our teachers tried, without success, to take it down. We would check the board and then gather in the school lot at 3 o'clock. Everyone would form a big circle and kids who had had a problem that day would get in there and punch each other until somebody gave up. This was how we ended each school day.

I feel lucky that I was only put in that position twice, the first time after I tried to repeat a joke I had heard at New York's Paramount Theater. My mom had taken me there to see Danny Kaye, and the opener was the black dance act "Tip, Tap, and Toe." As the dancers danced and sweated on stage, one said to the other, "White people sweat white milk, but we sweat chocolate milk!" I repeated this in class the next day. Of course, this was not particularly funny to my friend Leon Patton, the only black student in our class. So I ended up on the bulletin board for the fight of the day. The two of us didn't get very much punching in, and we ended it in the way most of these fights ended, by walking away not hating each other or bringing it back to class the next day.

I did have a problem with a kid named Fuzzy Sessa, a real bully who would come up to me every day and punch me in the arm. I was afraid of Fuzzy. It got to the point where he would ask me which arm I wanted to take the punch in. When I was twelve, I finally summoned up all the courage in my body and soul and waited him to ask me which arm. When I answered him with, "Neither, and don't try it!" he laughed at me, really laughed at me, but when he came to punch me I knocked him down! So once again my name went up on the bulletin board.

Fuzzy Sessa versus Rubber Belly Modell set for 3 o'clock. Everyone welcome! ("Rubber Belly" had become my nickname in seventh and eighth grade, because one day when playing punch-ball, the ball hit my belly and bounced out to second base!) It felt so good to kick the crap out of him that day. I am a lover, not a fighter, but I called on all the stuff that had been brewing for weeks, all the black-and-blue arms, and I gave it to Fuzzy.

He never bothered me again, nor did anyone else. Part of this is due to the fact that I had already started to play the trumpet. Whenever there was going to be a rumble, my pals would always tell me to get out before the fight started, so that I didn't get hit in the chops and be unable to play. When I think about it that was really nice of them. I was never a part of those rumbles.

But there was one time that I really feared for my life. I was playing in an open lot with my friends Georgie Ashcroft, a Catholic kid, and Mickey Gelb, who was Jewish. To our surprise, before we knew it, we were surrounded by a crowd of black guys armed with clubs and sticks. We weren't accustomed to any kind of racial tension, so we were totally unprepared for this.

In our neighborhood, in any kind of stand-off, the first question was always, "What religion are you?" If you knew what gang was asking you that, there were a couple of safe answers. Mickey Gelb replied, "I'm a Catholic." I took the other safe one, "I'm Christian." So here was poor Georgie Ashcroft, who really was Catholic, but we'd taken the two good choices, facing a young guy with a club in the air asking him, "And what are you?" With his whole body shaking, Georgie replied, "I'm a Mongolian!" At this, the guy just broke up laughing, along with everybody else. I was relieved that the gang walked away and left us alone because I thought we had really had it. I'll never forget the expression on Georgie Ashcroft's face and his great line, "I'm a Mongolian

My uncle Milty had attended James Monroe High School, so there were high musical expectations for me there. High school provided my first experience in being part of an ensemble, a kind of epiphany for me. Although the daily rehearsal in our Junior Band was mostly filled with scales and chords, the last ten minutes were devoted to playing easy marches from the composer VanderCook. Playing those marches really turned me on, and I became another person entirely when I played and connected with this musical ensemble.

After only one year of high school, I auditioned for the All-City Orchestra of New York. The auditioner was an elderly man named Charles Gartlan, superintendent of music for the New York City schools. We were asked to play the first trumpet part of Sibelius's "Finlandia." Mr. Gartlan pointed to a place in the music that was thick with black sixteenth notes, and I could not figure out the rhythm at all. Nor, at that time, could I double-tongue. After a few futile attempts, Mr. Gartlan looked at me and said, "I don't think you are suited for the trumpet. Perhaps the string bass would be better." In retrospect, I don't think the superintendent was aware of the power and position he held over students. Do we ever realize the kind of impact we as teachers can have on a child's life?

The very next week, at age fourteen, I auditioned for the All-City Band of New York and was given First Chair. Thereafter, every Saturday morning I would get on a train at Simpson Street in the Bronx, ride to 66th Street and Columbus Circle, right where Lincoln Center is now, and walk to Columbus High School to rehearse with the All-City Band. My mother would give me twenty-five cents—two nickels for the subway, one for each way, and fifteen cents for a treat! After our first few rehearsals, I met some guys in the band who suggested we pool our money and rent a studio for an hour to play big-band arrangements. This was my very first experience with big-band jazz. It was mostly Johnny Warrington charts, like "I'll Remember April" or "Moonlight in Vermont." I was excited to play lead trumpet in a new genre, especially when I had a written solo. These were glorious times, as well as superb training for my future musical career.

The following year I discovered the Bronx Symphony, a wonderful local community orchestra. We rehearsed on Tuesday evenings at Walton High School, under the baton of a very gifted conductor, Irwin Hoffman. The first piece I played was the overture to "The Barber of Seville," which was in A-trumpet. Due to my early training, I had no problem transposing it. The next piece, however, was Dvorak's "New World Symphony," in E-trumpet, and I was lost. I had not yet mastered that more difficult transposition. Hoffman stopped me after a few really bad mistakes and told me to come back when I could transpose the piece perfectly. In those early days, writing out the entire trumpet part for a B-flat trumpet saved me many times. It also improved my practice of transposing, which made things easier, especially when I was sight-reading.

During my high school years, I also played in four or five community orchestras, among them the Yonkers Philharmonic, the 92nd Street Orchestra, and the Washington Heights Symphony. What great training that was for me, learning the repertoire and getting the feel of being a principal player! My training was also enhanced by WQXR, a New York City radio station that played classical music twenty-four hours a day. Every night I went to sleep with the radio playing next to my ear, experiencing the entire classical music repertoire played by the world's great orchestras and the principal trumpeters of that time. This helped me immensely for future auditions.

As for my romantic education, in high school I had only one date in four years--Rosalie Lubin, a lovely young lady, asked me to take her to the senior prom. In high school, I was tremendously busy playing in a community orchestra almost every night of the week, and that made it hard to find the time to go out with girls. But I was also overweight and very aware of it. I had many good girl friends, all of whom regarded me as an older brother. I wish I had had the confidence to pursue them. I really wanted to! Although I was an extremely serious musician, my proclivity for ad-lib comedy got me into trouble during my senior year at James Monroe High School. Our economics teacher, Dr. Elizabeth Scanlon, was the stereotypical spinster. She was in her sixties, probably weighed around 250 pounds, and the black dresses she wore every day were not kind to her shape. Her hair was pulled back in a tight bun with a knitting needle through it. Dr. Scanlon was a very strict and demanding teacher, and at the end of one of our classes she assigned us a chapter on consumer cooperatives to read for the next day.

But that night, Rocky Marciano fought Joe Louis on TV, live from Yankee Stadium. This was a fight never to be forgotten, because we were all aghast to see Joe Louis, our hero and champion, knocked through the ropes by Rocky Marciano, his great career ending before our eyes.

When we came into class the next morning, Dr. Scanlon started asking us questions about consumer cooperatives. No one was answering a single question, and Dr. Scanlon got angry. Finally, all 250 pounds of her walked out from behind her desk, stood up in front of it, and with her hands on her hips, threatening, "I am going around this entire class with one question. God help you all if somebody can't answer it."

In every class I ever attended, you could count on three or four kids who always knew the answers to everything. Dr. Scanlon questioned each one of us, probably thirty students, but not one person could describe a consumer cooperative. Now she was really steaming. Hands on hips, she looked at our class and asked, "Are you all a bunch of morons? All the morons, stand up, please!" Well, nobody popped up. Five seconds later, I did, and she looked hard at me and said, "Modell! Do you think you are a moron?" I replied, "No, Dr. Scanlon, but I hate to see you standing there by yourself!"

The class went into an uproar. Dr. Scanlon grabbed me by the shirt and hauled me downstairs to Leo Taub, Dean of Boys at James Monroe High School. I knew him well because his son Richard was a timpanist, and we played together in the Bronx Symphony. It was funny to see Dr. Scanlon explaining to Dean Taub what I had said, and Dean Taub trying hard not to laugh. When Dr. Scanlon left, and the door closed, the dean looked at me asked, "Why do you always do this to me?"

Another adventure I remember vividly from high school involved the miracle of how I passed my senior history class. There were two fine history teachers at James Monroe that Sandy and I really admired—Don Waldman and Jess Witchell.

I took history with Don Waldman my senior year, and since I was playing in four community orchestras a minimum of four nights a week and rarely studying, it was not surprising that I was flunking his history class. Don Waldman, a nice man whom I liked very much, explained to me that as things stood, if I didn't make at least a 90 on the final exam, I would fail the course and be unable to graduate. In order to make sure I wouldn't be tempted to cheat on my exam, Mr. Waldman had me sit in the last seat of the last row, with not a single soul near me. My grade for the final exam turned out to be 92.

Several years after graduation, I came back to Monroe to visit, and I made sure I stopped to see Don Waldman. We are not always proud of everything we have done in life, and I had desperately needed to graduate. Don Waldman looked at me and said bluntly, "Okay. How did you do it?" What he meant, of course, was how in the world I had managed to score a 92 when prior to that it had been a string of 30s and 40s and 60s. I replied, "If you remember back to that day, I had a very bad cold." "Yeah," Waldman remembered, "you kept taking your . . .handkerchief . . .out." I'd written all the information I could cram on my handkerchief! So that is how I passed history and graduated from James Monroe.

Passing the economics final turned into a real scandal. My friend Diane, an excellent student who always made the honor roll, worked in the Economics Department office, and she gave me a copy of the final. Not being a snob, I naturally had shared it with all of my friends. On the morning of the final our principal, Dr. Henry Hein, made me stand up and take a bow during an all school assembly, when he announced that I had just been awarded a small scholarship to the University of Miami in Coral Gables.

Later on in class, we heard through the loudspeaker, "Would you please send Ronald Modell down to Dr. Hein's office?" I thought for sure I was being sent to get more laudatory comments, perhaps a pat on the back. But when I walked in, Dr. Hein closed the door and looked a me intently: "Your name," he said, "has come up in the economics final scandal. We know that you were the second person to get a copy of the test, and we have already backtracked and found all the people to whom you passed it on. All I want to know is, how did you get it? If you can't tell me that," he concluded gravely, "I am going to have to suspend you and you are not going to graduate." Graduation was only a few weeks away.

I just couldn't turn in my friend Diane. It would have been a complete disaster for her life. I refused to tell, even though I was threatened right up until graduation. I never did reveal who it was.

On Graduation Day the temperature was 108 degrees, a blistering day for us dressed in our full caps and gowns in a high school without air conditioning. When I was called up to share the music medal, the principal shook my hand and told me congratulations. But the last words Dr. Henry Hein ever said to me were, "Who was it?" I only replied, "Thank you very much," took my medal, and walked off the stage.

FIRST GIGS, LEARNING AND EARNING

My very first professional engagement came as a freshman in high school. It was during the Jewish holidays in September, and my parents were out of town in their bungalow in Oakland, New Jersey. I had stayed home in the Bronx for the weekend to play my first gig, a Sunday night Bar Mitzvah. We lived in the East Bronx, and when you looked out our window—we were one story up—there was a Jewish deli right across on the corner, next to it a candy store, and then a whole slew of stores where we regularly shopped. On a Sunday night, however, they were all closed and dark. The Bar Mitzvah was two subway stops from my house, scheduled for eight o'clock.

I put on the only suit I owned, and then discovered I could only find a nickel and three pennies—subway fare was a dime. Frantically I started looking through my mom and dad's dresser, ransacking the kitchen as panic started to set in. All the stores were closed, and it was getting to be twenty minutes to eight. I looked out our window and suddenly remembered seeing my mother wrap two or three pennies in a napkin and drop it into the yard for some struggling itinerant musicians.

Still in a frenzy, I took off my good suit, put on a pair of torn jeans with a big hole in the knee, pulled on an old shirt, took down my trumpet, and raced down to the yard. I started to play, and after only a few notes a napkin came sailing down with three cents in it! I took the pennies, pocketed them, ran upstairs, got back into my suit, and raced to the subway station on Hunts Point Avenue. I had an extra penny! At the subway stop there were yellow machines selling chocolate for a penny: milk chocolate, dark chocolate, chocolate with nuts. I spent my last penny on dark chocolate, which I have always loved, and still do.

My first serious steady gig came in 1950 in the Catskill Mountains, a popular Jewish resort area north of New York City. There, the season started on the July Fourth weekend and ended at Labor Day. My first two summers playing in the Catskills were based at the Steirs Hotel in Ferndale, a wonderful small hotel that housed a hundred guests. While I would later perform at a hotel for 3500 guests, my summers at Steirs were special and intimate.

Our staff living quarters, however, were wretched. The staff dining room, however, served the same food as the hotel dining room, and we ate like kings! Food has traditionally been one of the main attractions at Catskills hotels.

Our group performed six days a week, with Mondays off. There were five of us: a pianist, a tenor saxophonist, alto saxophonist, myself on trumpet and a drummer. We played dance music all six nights, but on Friday and Saturday nights the hotel featured variety shows that included a dance team, a vocalist and a comedian.

I think that during our first year in 1950 we probably ruined more acts than any other band in the Catskills. None of us had any experience—although our dance music was fine. But none of us knew what a first or second ending was, or a *del segno* sign, or anything else that you needed to know in order to perform a show. The Catskills, however, were a great place to play in the musical minor leagues.

Other beginning performers featured were future greats Joey Bishop, Buddy Hackett, Lenny Bruce, and Jerry Lewis, who actually worked as a bellhop at Browns Hotel. Sid Caesar had a summer gig playing the sax.

During the 1950s, the Catskills were still attracting great performers from New York's famous Second Avenue Theater, a landmark of Jewish entertainment. Catskill audiences were treated to the performances of veterans like Michel Rosenberg, with his classic bit about a Jewish man going to his first major-league baseball game, or marvelous singing teams like Esta Saltzman and David Lubritski, or Henrietta Jacobsen and Julius Adler. Two of the greatest names in Jewish theater history were comedian Menasha Skulnik and Molly Picon, who later became well-known playing the matchmaker in "Fiddler on the Roof." It was a memorable experience to play the music from the Second Avenue Theater. You couldn't buy that experience.

By the second summer, the band was back, and we were terrific. One summer's experience had really given us the tools we needed, and now we were an outstanding show band. To illustrate the contrast between these two summers, two incidents in particular stand out, one very funny and one not so funny.

Early in the season that first summer, the hotel featured a roller skating team called the Flying Hurricanes. They told us they would be using a neck swivel for their grand finale, a tricky maneuver where the man would start spinning the woman rapidly around his neck. When they reached a certain speed, at that point in the music we were to slow down until they gradually came to a halt. But we messed up! We kept playing and playing at top speed until those poor people couldn't stand up straight. When we realized our mistake and mercifully stopped the music, they were falling all over themselves and could barely stand. Clearly our band had a lot to learn.

The following year, more seasoned and more confident, we did a show with a very popular comedian, Eddie Schaefer. He drank a lot. Eddie was a big, tall man, and he did a bit called "Sam, You Made the Pants Too Long," which Fannie Brice had made famous. I remember distinctly during an afternoon rehearsal that Eddie Schaefer told us, no matter what he said, no matter how he carried on, that we were not to stop playing until he gave us the word cue "chutzpah."

It seems Eddie had been drinking prior to the show, and when we reached the critical part of the act, he could not remember the word cue for us to stop the music. He was beside himself, yet he had been explicit during rehearsal that no matter how he acted we were not to stop playing. After I don't know how long—and five minutes on stage feels like an eternity—the band realized that he had truly forgotten the word, and we stopped. At this point, Eddie looked at the audience in the Steirs Hotel Playhouse and said, "Do you see those five schmucks back there?" At that, the five of us got up, walked out to center stage, turned our rear ends around, and yelled, "Kish Mein Tuchus!"—kiss my ass—before walking off stage. Eddie was forced to finish his act without any music. Reflecting on it now, I think it took a lot of chutzpah, (a lot of nerve), for us to do that. It showed our confidence in the way we felt we performed as a band, as *profesionals*. It was not our mistake; it was his mistake!

My two summers at Steirs Hotel were special. Because it was a small hotel, you got to know everybody, every guest and all their children. Each day I would play baseball with the hotel guests' kids and swim with them in the pool. It was so much more fun than playing at hotels like the Concord, the Pines, or Grossinger's, where there could be thousands of guests, and you would never get to know any of them.

For my third summer in the Catskills, I was engaged at the Golden Hotel in Hurleyville. After only a few days, the elderly Jewish man who owned it came up to me and said, "I have to let you go because you are too good for this place." What he really meant was that I couldn't play the old Jewish *freilach* his guests preferred to contemporary dance music. It was the first time I was fired for being too good! But I was immediately hired by British bandleader Johnny Danser, based at the Woodlawn Villa at Lake Koenaga. We had a wonderful little group, playing the required dance music and also featuring some really great jazz, which most hotels did not permit their musicians to play. It turned out to be a nice finish to the summer.

The one summer I didn't play in the Catskills was in 1955, which I spent in Dallas at the Baker Hotel. Our four-piece band played in the Mural Room, led by Pierson Thal, a well-known bandleader and pianist. It was one of those exclusive places where the musicians were instructed to come out, play their set, and walk off stage—never to fraternize with the guests, who tended to be Dallas's elite. If a guest were to talk to you, you were to answer politely but get out of the room as fast as you could. Nonetheless, it was a fun gig because every two weeks we featured a different artist. We started with Matty Melnick, a Hollywood composer and violinist who had written the hit "Stairway to the Stars."He was followed by singer Russell Arms, then appearing on a nationally televised show, "Your Hit Parade."

One night one of Dallas's most famous strippers, Miss Candy Barr, came sauntering through the hotel lobby in her cowgirl outfit. Miss Barr had platinum blonde hair and was packing two pearl-handled pistols! She had dropped by to see our show with Russell Arms. When our show was over, she asked Russell if he would come across the street to see her midnight show at Abe's Colony Club (the same club frequented by the notorious Jack Ruby). I was twenty-one years old when Russell Arms asked me, "Do you want to come and watch Candy Barr strip?" Of course I did.

We were seated ringside and my expectations of Miss Barr were running high. But first was an opening act, a vocal group who came out and completely overwhelmed me, singing harmonies like I had never heard before—arrangements that were so striking that when they finished, and Candy Barr came out to strip for Russell Arms right in front of our table, I have no memory of it. That may be difficult to believe for a young man as horny and hard-up as I was. I had heard a new group, just breaking in; that would eventually become the Hi-Los, probably one of the greatest vocal groups of its time, or even of all time. The next day I called everybody I knew musically in New York to share my new discovery. The Hi-Los went on to a brilliant career as sophisticated jazz vocalists, and I was not surprised.

Still another highlight of that summer were the frequent visits to our nightclub by a very distinguished older gentleman, probably around seventy years old, who would arrive at night escorted on each arm by a different gorgeous young woman. I, of course, wanted to know who he was, and I found out his name was Nick and that he owned one of the best restaurants in the entire country. One night after our set, when the two young ladies had gone to the powder room, I passed Nick's table and he motioned me to come over. We introduced ourselves, and he said, "Boy, I don't know what it is that I have, but these young chicks just come at me like I'm a magnet!" I was thinking to myself, well, the money you have, the restaurant. Nick invited the band out one night to have dinner at his fabulous house. It was way out of town, and when you drove into the driveway of his big ranch home, there were four Cadillacs parked there—a Coup de Ville, a Sedan de Ville, an Eldorado, and a Fleetwood. One each side of every fender, in solid gold, was emblazoned the name "Nick."

A week or two later, Nick invited me to dinner at his restaurant, where we sat in his private booth. The maitre d' came and gave us the menu. My mother, I remembered, had always told me that when you are invited out as a guest, never order the most expensive thing. So I procrastinated, looking and looking until finally Nick told the maitre d' "Bring this boy the best steak in the house; make it one of those Kansas City sirloins."

I then proceeded to commit the three most awful mistakes you can make when eating in a place like Nick's. First, I asked for my steak to be well-done. Then, when it arrived, I requested ketchup. Finally, I didn't know how to cut the steak properly. Through all of this, Nick was very sweet and didn't say a word, until our steaks were finished, and we were on the dessert course. Then he looked at me and said, "Young man, if in the future you are given an invitation to this type of restaurant, may I tell you that you NEVER EVER order your steak well-done; you NEVER EVER ask for ketchup; and you NEVER EVER cut a piece of meat like that." Good lessons, and I did remember in the future that ordering ketchup in a fine steakhouse is tantamount to asking a pastry chef to use a commercial cake mix instead of making the cake from scratch.

In the spring of 1956 I was introduced to Syd Sayre, a unique agent who booked bands in hotels throughout the Catskills. Syd offered me a job as leader of my own quintet for the entire off-season, from April to July, describing it in detail: "I am sending you up to the Stevensville Lake Hotel, where you'll be playing six days a week. Sunday, Tuesday, Wednesday, and Thursday you are going to be playing in the lobby, probably for only thirty or forty people. On Fridays and Saturdays there will be conventions coming up, where you may have a thousand people, and you will do a show both nights in the playhouse, followed by a late show in the lounge area. The second show will feature a belly dancer, so on Saturdays be prepared to work your ass off. Mondays you'll be off."

By the spring of 1956, I was a seasoned trumpet player and feeling pretty good about myself. For the first time, I was assuming all the duties and responsibilities of a bandleader. On our very first night playing in the lobby, we started with standard show tunes, then mixed in some waltzes, rumbas, and popular songs of the day. As we were playing, I noticed a man standing off to the side with a big cigar in his mouth, puffing away. We played a 45-minute set, and then I called a break. I had just put my trumpet in its case when the cigar-smoking man came up to me. His name was Harry Dinnerstein, and he owned the hotel. He also owned a huge resort hotel in Miami, the Beau Rivage, so I imagine he was pretty wealthy.

His very first words to me, as I left the piano area, after conducting my first set ever as a leader and as a trumpet player, were "Hey kid! You stink!" I was floored. Then he asked me, "How come you don't all play at the same time, the five of youse?" I managed to say, "Well, the routine is that we start the tune, and I play the first part of the melody, the saxophone plays the middle of the song, then I come back, and then we let him play a little bit . . ." He interrupted me, ordering "I paid for five musicians, and I want five musicians playing at all times cuz that's what I paid for!"

Harry Dinnerstein turned out to be not the greatest guy to work for. Like most hotel owners in the Catskills, he watched every penny. I remember the time Harry Dinnerstein wouldn't allow bread to be served in our staff dining room. I assume he was trying to save the hotel some money. So I asked the waiter why we couldn't get any, and his response was, "Mr. Dinnerstein said no bread for the band tonight." I told him, "Well, you go tell Mr. Dinnerstein that if the band doesn't get any bread, the band will not perform tonight. And the waiter came back a few minutes later with a plate of bread.

Clever though he was, Harry Dinnerstein met his match in Charlie Rapp, the most formidable theatrical agent in the Catskills. Charlie booked entertainment for the Catskills' largest hotels. He and Dinnerstein played a game where each thought they were outfoxing the other.

On Monday mornings, Charlie would send Dinnerstein a bill for the previous week's entertainment. If a dance team's actual cost was $350, Charlie Rapp would charge Dinnerstein $500. If the singer cost $600, Charlie Rapp would charge him $800, a comedian costing $1000 would be billed to Dinnerstein for $1250. I overheard Dinnerstein telling his secretary, "You know, that dance team ain't worth no $500. Give 'em three-fifty." Same with the singer: "Don't give him no $800. He ain't worth more than six hundred." Charlie Rapp had figured out Dinnerstein's math, and they made sure he always arrived at the figure he wanted. For all his cleverness, this was one of the times when Dinnerstein was not as clever as he thought.

That spring, in 1956, I did a show conducting for a new comedian named Jackie Vernon, playing in a large playhouse that could seat up to a thousand people. This was the only time in my entire career of playing hundreds of shows, that I ever saw an act in which a comedian did not get one single laugh the entire evening.

It made no difference that he had the band behind him convulsed. His material was hip and new, but his brilliant deadpan delivery obviously made no connection with the older Jewish guests. One of his lines that night I remember is, "The height of self-confidence—General Custer at Little Bighorn turning to his captain and saying, 'Don't take any prisoners.'" The band was in hysterics—but nobody in the audience laughed. They sat in stony silence with their arms folded. He went on to a fine career in comedy and is still nationally known each Christmas as the voice of Frosty the Snowman.

The Stevensville Lake Hotel off season gig was an important learning experience for me. On July 4th, the official summer season began. Mac Pollack, the hotel's show band conductor, asked me to play second trumpet with the brilliant trumpeter Murray Rothstein. Our piano player was Warner Shilkret, and Mel Zelnick was on drums, they both occasionally played for Skitch Henderson's Tonight Show band. Playing in the Catskills was a marvelous opportunity for many musicians to bring their families with them. Without a doubt, this was the best show band I would play with in the Catskills. Murray Rothstein was phenomenal. I can't express how much I admired him, as a lead player, a jazz player, and a Klezmer musician. Murray was also one of the best club date trumpet players in New York City. Although my main job was playing first trumpet in the Latin band, the experience of being part of this incredible show band is a vivid memory I carry to this day.

One night a well-known singer, who had brought along her own trumpet player, performed a slow blues number and for the first time I heard a technique known as a "slow Basie shake." What a marvelous effect! It thrilled me to death. When the show was over, I couldn't wait to ask this visiting trumpeter, "How did you do that?" I was twenty-two years old and dying to know. He just turned to me and said, "Learn yourself, punk." Or in other words, "I am not going to tell you anything that could make you as good as me or near as good as me cuz then you might steal a gig from me." That was the general mindset in the music field at that time. Thank God this has changed. Many, many times I have watched Maynard Ferguson, James Moody, Louie Bellson, or Dizzy Gillespie, sitting with aspiring students for hours, answering every single question to the best of their abilities.

At Stevensville, we would play dance music after every show and our musicians would take turns playing marvelously improvised solos. But I was very frustrated. I wanted to be able to improvise, but I couldn't; I didn't know how, didn't know the first thing about improvisation. So one afternoon I went to our Latin pianist, Louie White, in Bobby Madera's band, and asked him, "Could you write out a chorus of 'Jeepers Creepers'" in the key of C, so when we fake it tonight, I'll ask if I can play an improvised solo?" The way this works, you play the melody one time through, and then the second time, you improvise. I practiced like crazy and got this "improvisation" solo to where I could really feel I was improvising—even though they weren't my notes; it was all Louie White's.

Then came my big night. I asked Mac Pollack if I could play a chorus on "Jeepers Creepers." Well, the band thought, let's really put it to this twenty-two year old kid. After we played the first chorus in C, I stood up proudly to play my solo, not realizing that the entire band had gone into the key of B, a half tone lower. When I started to play my solo, it sounded horrible! The half-step discrepancy created all kinds of terrible dissonances. I kept looking at the music; I knew it had sounded fine with Louie on the piano. Halfway through the tune, the band couldn't stand it any longer. They started cracking up, and I realized what they had done. It was total embarrassment, and I walked off the bandstand that night with my tail between my legs.

I didn't know how I was going to get my revenge, but I knew that I was going to get it. A few weeks later, while we were playing

"How Deep is the Ocean," I had a four-bar solo just playing the melody, and I had played the same notes night after night. I went to Julie Schwartz, lead alto and a great improviser and said, "Julie, would you allow me the opportunity to get these bastards back, and write me a four-bar solo the same way Dizzy Gillespie would have played those four bars?" This was a straight ballad, so no one would ever expect anything that far out.

I gotta tell you; it was one of the biggest thrills of my life! When it was my turn to stand up and play, where these guys were so used to hearing me play the plain old melody, I broke into this incredible four-bar solo with lots of notes, and it sounded fantastic. Every member of that band turned around and looked at me, and as I finished the last note, the middle finger on my right hand went straight up in the air, at every one of them, as I yelled good naturedly, "Fuck you!"

SERVING THE QUEEN:
ON TOUR WITH CORNELIA OTIS SKINNER

In June 1952 when I graduated from James Monroe High School, I had been awarded a small scholarship to the University of Miami in Coral Cables, provided that I would play first trumpet in the Miami Philharmonic. Three days before I was scheduled to leave, my mother had gone out and purchased a Florida wardrobe for me, something they honestly could not afford. The afternoon we returned from shopping; my uncle Milty called to tell there was to be an audition for a Broadway show that would tour the United States for eight-and-a-half months. After conferring with my uncle Louis, they both agreed that if I promised to go to college the following year, they would allow me to audition.

The day of the audition there were four of five other trumpet players whom I heard warming up, and after chatting with some of them I discovered they were Broadway-experienced. I was barely seventeen-and-a-half yet had the moxie to think, "bring it on."

Young as I was, I was unaware of the reputation of the conductor, Nathaniel Shilkret. I was to learn more about him as the tour progressed. Despite my lack of Broadway experience, Nat Shilkret apparently heard something in my playing, and I won the audition.

Afterwards, my uncle Milty and I waited by the phone on a Sunday morning for the official offer with my contract details. When the phone finally rang, and with my uncle Milty listening in, I was offered the position at $154 a week. Up until that time, the most money I had ever made was $27.55 a week in the Catskill Mountains. My uncle's hand covered the receiver, and he whispered to me, you can't go for less than $175 a week. With my mouth wide open in disbelief, I asked him, "Are you crazy?" He said, "Do what I tell you to do," so, with real sadness in my voice, I said, "I can't go for less than $175 a week." The conductor said he would have to call me back in five minutes. Those five minutes seemed like five years to me, but he did call back and said that would be just fine.

The show, "Paris 90," was a one-woman show starring Cornelia Otis Skinner, who also wrote the show in collaboration with Samuel Taylor. Miss Skinner portrayed fifteen different types of women found in 1890 Paris, beginning with a British nanny, quickly shifting to a Spanish duchess, a loose French woman, a Boston lesbian schoolteacher. All were delivered in impeccably perfect accents. Twelve of the characters were written as comedy, but Miss Skinner captivated the audience with her three remaining dramatic characters. My particular favorite was in Act III, when she portrayed five of the characters painted by Henri de Toulouse Lautrec.

Cornelia Otis Skinner was hands down the greatest at doing any accent. I would be sitting in the orchestra pit, watching in disbelief, unable to accept that all these totally distinctive characters were actually played by one actress. The score, written in the style of French composer Jacques Offenbach (famous for his can-can), was by prominent female composer Kay Swift, who had written the hit song, "Fine and Dandy." Our company carried three key musicians—trumpet, violin, and piano—and in each city we would add eight local musicians.

The tour began in mid-September of 1952 in Schenectady, New York with a morning rehearsal, an afternoon matinee, and an evening performance. After the matinee, in what was to become my modus operandi, I went directly to Cornelia Otis Skinner's dressing room and knocked on her door. As the door opened, I thought I was seeing the Queen, tall and stately, dressed in a beautiful robe, truly the picture of royalty. She looked at me and said "Yes?" to which I replied, "Hi, I'm Ronnie Modell, your trumpet player for the next eight-and-a-half months, and I thought we should get to know each other." How much chutzpah was that?

Evidently she loved it, for from that point on we had a close relationship until the day she died. During the entire tour, Miss Skinner would have me come in every evening, ninety minutes before curtain, to sit in her dressing room while she applied her makeup, and we told each other how our days had gone.

After that first day, we went to Montreal for one week and then on to Toronto. I must tell you that all the veteran theater people traveling with this show told me I was being spoiled rotten as we had our own Pullman car for the entire tour. Train travel back then was superb; the food was elegant and served as you would have been served in the finest restaurant.

It was my first time in my own train compartment, and the old veterans enjoyed playing practical jokes on me. The first time we were on an overnight trip, I asked one of the old timers about changing into my pajamas in my tiny sleeping compartment. They told me, "You have to do it lying on your bed. I know that's uncomfortable, but there's no other way." So there I was, struggling to get my clothes off, lying in that netted bed, and found out the following day that you're supposed to go to the men's room with your pajamas and change there. They all had a big laugh at my expense, and there was to be more of that during the tour.

The night we got on the train in Toronto to go to Boston, our conductor Nat Shilkret came and got me, as Ms. Skinner had requested my presence. Nat and I stepped into her compartment, where she sat propped up in bed in her pajamas, and she said to me "Now Ronnie, Nat tells me that you know the cutest dirty jokes, and I would love to hear some." Once again, the history of my joke-telling goes back a long way.

I have always had a phenomenal memory, and while we were appearing in Atlanta I turned eighteen years old. After the show, the Atlanta musical contractor invited the entire company to his home to celebrate my birthday. There was lots of food and much to drink. At one point during the evening, Ms. Skinner was lying on the floor on her back and doing some sort of trick with her nose and a twenty-five cent piece. But the highlight of the party came when to the astonishment of the entire company, I performed from memory all the characters in Paris 90.

The two days we spent in Denver allowed Ms. Skinner to take her wardrobe mistress, Marie Mann, and myself up into the Colorado Rockies to show us the cabin where she did a lot of her writing. We drove up into the mountains in a car Ms. Skinner had rented, through some of the most breath-taking scenery in America. When we reached our destination, Ms. Skinner said, "So, what did you think, Ronnie?" To which I replied, "Oh it just looked like a bunch of hills and mountains to me." When I think back to this, what strikes me is how much I was still a kid from the Bronx.

As we neared our engagement at the Blackstone Theater in Chicago, Ms. Skinner said to me, "Now Ronnie, there is a lady that writes for the *Chicago Tribune* named Claudia Cassidy. She's probably not going to like our show, but under no circumstances do I want you to go and see her or call, no matter what she writes." By this time, Ms. Skinner was well aware of my chutzpah, as well as my deep affection for her. She knew I was not above picking up the phone and expressing my feelings about her review.

The tour concluded in Washington, D.C. in April 1953. My relationship with Ms. Skinner continued. We saw each other next during her Broadway performance in "Major Barbara." I attended a rehearsal there one day and had the thrill of meeting two of my favorite actors, Charles Laughton and Burgess Meredith. When Ms. Skinner introduced me to Charles Laughton as her former trumpet player, he immediately asked me to show him how to form his lips to play a trombone, which was part of his character in the show.

It really is true that youth is wasted on the young. Remembering all the wonderful experiences on that tour, I have wished many times during my life that I could do it again, knowing what I know now. Ms. Skinner and I corresponded for many years after the show, and she gave me the great honor of accepting my firstborn son Scott to be her godson.

THE LATIN YEARS: RICO CALIENTE Y SABROSO!

During the late 50's, Latin music was all the rage, and Jewish people were some of its biggest fans. I've now come to realize that my great affinity and love for Latin music stems from its shared roots with Jewish music. Even my mother's parents grasped this. The first time I played them a recording of a Spanish street singer from Malaga, they were convinced it was a Jewish cantor.

In the summer of 1957, I played lead trumpet in the show band at the Pines Hotel, which also featured a popular Latin band, the Joe Cuba Sextet. That summer Joe would ask both me and the other trumpet player in our band to sit in with his sextet. His band was getting a lot of attention because of its hit record, "Cuando Paso"—it was absolutely, as they say in Spanish, "rico caliente y sabroso," red, hot, and sensual.

Our trumpet playing made a big impact on Joe Cuba, so much so that he had arrangements written to expand his sextet to an octet that now included two trumpets. We were a big part of giving him that big-band Latin sound. After that summer, Joe Cuba engaged me to keep playing with his band.

One gig I will never forget was our date at Rockland Palace, near the old Polo Grounds where the New York Giants baseball team played. The gig ran from eleven at night to three in the morning, so traveling to that part of the Bronx was then a bit dangerous. My dad took me there in his cab, telling me, "I will drop you off, but then you're on your own." I was playing there with another trumpet player, Bruce Paster, whom I had known since high school. We walked into the Rockland Palace and found we were the only white faces. It was shocking for us, for the first time to be in the minority! I remember walking up to Jimmy Sabater, the timbale player with Joe Cuba, who was a dark-complexioned man from Puerto Rico. I said to him, "Jimmy! Stay close to me, man, I'm scared!" Jimmy said to me, "Hey, don't be scared, man, they hate us worse than they hate you!" Around two thousand people were there that night, and the opening act was the Horace Silver Quintet, featuring Art Farmer and Hank Mobley. We followed them at midnight, and at one in the morning came the Dizzy Gillespie big band. Dizzy's band, featured

Lee Morgan, James Moody, Frank Rehak, and Charlie Persip. At two a.m., Bruce and I were in a taxi on our way home from one of the most exciting nights in my career. It was an evening not to be forgotten.

In 1958 show bandleader Marty Beck engaged me for the summer at the Concord Hotel to play third trumpet in his band. But the real reason I was hired was because I had symphonic experience and knew the repertoire of the Jewish theater. Every Wednesday, the renowned composer and conductor of the Jewish theater, Sholom Secunda, would bring up some of New York City's finest symphonic musicians to augment the show band. To the great delight of the hotel guests, we would present a concert of classical and Jewish music.

The Concord was the number one hotel in the Catskills, which gave me the opportunity to play with some of the real legends in show business. That summer the Concord opened its new Cordillion Room, an enormous nightclub that could accommodate 3500 guests. Joey Bishop opened on the first night.

But it was on the second night that I enjoyed one of the funniest moments in my entire professional life. The opening act for headliner Harry Belafonte was the unique ventriloquist Senor Wences. He had appeared many times on the Ed Sullivan show, taking out a white glove and drawing a face on his right hand, talking to this imaginary character, Topo Gigio (the mouse). Senor Wences also had a cigar box that when opened, revealed the head of a man who would bark out "Ees all right!" At rehearsal Senor Wences told the band leader that he did not have music, but that all he needed was for the band to fake "Lady of Spain" to bring him on. Once he reached the microphone and the applause died down; we were to cut the music. At the end, when he finished and said good night, we were to repeat "Lady of Spain" as his exit music.

We rehearsed that for a few minutes as we waited for Harry Belafonte. All of Belafonte's dancers and singers were there in full costume, and we all waited and waited. I thought nobody was looking at me, and I sidled up to where Senor Wences' cigar box sat. I had no idea that he was following me from the time I left the bandstand and started toward that cigar box. When I thought no one was watching, I gently opened the box, and as soon as I had it open, the great ventriloquist went, "Eeees all right!" I think I nearly wet my pants. By that time, everybody had noticed what was going on, and they all broke into laughter. I was the laughing fool of the day.

The Concord Hotel employed five bands. Their Latin band in 1958 was the fabulous Machito and his Afro-Cuban Orchestra. Machito was truly the father of all the Latin bands—Tito Puente, Tito Rodriguez, Eddie Palmieri, Charlie Palmieri had all been in his band, before breaking out on their own.

Machito had come from Cuba and was both a fantastic maracas player and a marvelous vocalist. He was also one of the legendary *soneros*, or "storytellers" ever. Many times I saw Machito do his thing: in the middle of his song he would adjust the lyrics and improvise a whole story about the people that he recognized dancing in front of him. The true leader of the Machito orchestra was another legend, trumpeter/alto saxophonist Mario Bauza. His story is astonishing and displays his sheer genius. A graduate of the Conservatory of Havana in clarinet and saxophone, Bauza had arrived in New York and struggled to find work. A friend of his told him of a band with a recording date in fifteen days that was in desperate need for a trumpeter. In just fifteen days, Mario Bauza taught himself the trumpet so well that before long he was engaged as the lead trumpet with the great Chick Webb Orchestra.

Still another trumpet-playing legend, Doc Cheatham, was part of the Machito orchestra that summer. Mario Bauza came to me one day and said, "You know, I saw you at the Palladium with Joe Cuba. Doc Cheatham is ill and will be out for a week—would you consider playing for Doc each night after you're done playing dance music with the show band? Just take off your tuxedo jacket and put on this," handing me a jacket in a vibrant Mexican print. I instantly responded "Oh, it would be my honor!

There were a host of well known writers who had written for Machito, including his pianist, Rene Hernandez, who wrote a lot of his charts, and they were fantastic. The rhythm section was made up of the timbale player, Ubaldo, Joe Mangual on bongos, and conga player

Carlos "Potato" Valdez. Graciela, our vocalist, was one of the great female Latin vocalists. Playing Latin music with Machito was as big a thrill as doing Mahler's Fourth Symphony, under Georg Solti's baton.

When Doc Cheatham returned, the first thing he did was to hand me his check for the week. I was astonished. This was the summer of 1958, and at those big resort hotels you were given room and board. I looked at the check and saw that the net take after taxes was $70. Shocked, I handed it right back to him, telling him, "Hey it was a great honor and an enormous pleasure for me to have played with this great orchestra." At the end of the summer, Doc quit the band and Mario Bauza asked me if I would take his place. For the next year, although we didn't work steadily, we did put together my first recording, "Vacation at the Concord," a collection of dance music we played that summer.

By the way, Latin music was never called "Salsa." As Tito Puente put it, "You eat salsa, but you play mambo, meringue, and cha cha." Every night the last thing we performed was a *Guajira*, which is the most beautiful, sexy, slow Latin dance. The saxophones would start a little riff, and then Mario Bauza would play what we call a *montuno* or improvised solo. There is no way to describe what you feel as a musician when music like that is being played at the very best level it can be played.

An amazing fact about my Latin years is that, unlike most other musicians, I never smoked marijuana. In fact, as I write this at age seventy-eight, I have yet to hold a marijuana cigarette in my hand. It has nothing to do with being for or against it. It is rather that when I was in high school, I was stricken with pneumonia and had to lie in bed for six weeks. To pass the time, I listened to the radio. The first federal drug hearings were being broadcast daily. It was all about addicts, and I heard kids talk about what it was like to need a fix, and not being able to get one. I became aware of the misery, pain, and suffering. Their stories suggested one started with marijuana and invariably graduated to heroin. Some of the kids that testified talked about going to the Star Theater on Southern Boulevard, the very same place where Sandy and I used to go every Saturday. So it really hit home. It scared the shit out of me, so that I was never tempted to have any drug of any sort.

Drugs were easily available to me when I joined the Latin bands, particularly Joe Cuba's band. The first year I played with Joe Cuba at the Pines; there was a raid one afternoon. I had never seen this happen before. Cars streamed into where the band's quarters were at the back of the Playhouse and quickly surrounded them. Federal drug agents took away our bass player and tore the place apart. This incident sealed the deal for me, and I decided that I never wanted to be involved in any of it, no matter who offered it to me. I was always grateful that in both Machito and Joe Cuba's bands nobody ever tried to challenge my "No, thank you" and tempt me to smoke.

Going back to 1956 every Wednesday night the Stevensville Lake Hotel would present "Mambo Jamboree," featuring some of the world's best Latin dancers, who demonstrated the hottest Latin dance steps for our guests. Of all the Latin dancers, none were better than Cuban Pete, with his partner Millie. On Wednesdays, in front of up to a thousand people, they would demonstrate the cha cha, meringue, and mambo.

I was trying to learn Spanish because I so loved singing Spanish songs. One night we were playing "Mambo del Pinguino," or the "mambo of the penguin." When we got to the chorus we sang, *Baile, baile como el Pinguino*. *Baile* means to swing, or dance, a penguin dance. In the middle of his mambo exhibition with Millie, Cuban Pete started to laugh so hard that he had to stop dancing. The band stopped playing, and Cuban Pete ran over to our bandleader Carlos Segui. They spoke rapidly in Spanish, and then Carlos Segui came over to me. "Gordito," he said to me, using my nickname which meant "The Little Fat One," "Gordito, sing to me what you just sang into the microphone." I proceeded to sing, *Baile baile como el pingo, baile baile*. "Gordito," he asked me, "don't you know what you just sang?" You see, *pinguino* was too hard a word for me to say, so it was easier to just cut it down to "pingo." "Gordito," said Carlos Segui, "you just sang, 'Swing, swing, swing your cock! No more *pingo*, huh? *Pinguino!*"

TULSA: MY SIX WONDERFUL YEARS AS AN OKIE

I had promised my two uncles that after touring with Cornelia Otis Skinner I would begin college the following year, and now I had to make good on that. During the Skinner tour, I had had the good fortune to audition for three of the world's best conductors, Eugene Ormandy (Philadelphia), Geroge Szell (Cleveland), and Leopold Stokowski, all at the tender age of eighteen-and-a-half. In my Philadelphia audition with Maestro Ormandy, he appeared with a stack of first-trumpet parts that took an hour-and-a-half to get through. At that point, Dvorak's "New World Symphony" was the most challenging piece I had ever played, so you can imagine my boldness in thinking, "Bring it on, I'll play it!"

We started with Richard Strauss's "Symphony Domestica." All I owned at that time was a pre-war medium-bore B-flat French Besson trumpet. To play for Ormandy some of the most demanding pieces in the repertoire—including "Don Juan," "Don Quixote," "Thus Spake Zarathustra," "Pictures at an Exhibition," and "La Mer"—required the nerve and moxie of an eighteen-year-old. After each excerpt, Maestro Ormandy would ask me, "Have you played this before?" My answer was always, "No."

At the conclusion of my audition, the Maestro told me, "You are very gifted, but you must find a smaller orchestra and spend three-to-five years learning the repertoire. Then I would like you to call me." (This was also the advice I heard when I auditioned for George Szell and Leopold Stokowski.) At that point, I would be ready for one of the Big Five--the orchestras of New York, Chicago, Philadelphia, Cleveland, or Boston.

I knew immediately what Ormandy was asking in terms of his advice to master the repertoire. I had first begun to hear "the repertoire" as a young boy when my uncles were visiting, and I would hear pieces like "Petroushka," or "Pictures at an Exhibition," repertoire standards for anyone desiring to become a symphonic trumpeter. I believe every genre of music has its own repertoire of pieces that you must know as well as your own name. In jazz, "Giant Steps," "Cherokee," "All the Things You Are," and "A Night in Tunisia" are part of the repertoire. If you perform at an Italian wedding, you had better know the "Tarentela,"

"Come Back to Sorrento," "O Sole Mio," and "Arrivederci Roma." Every one of these tunes became part of my multi-faceted repertoire, so that during those years when the symphony season was short, I was able to make a living.

Finally, as I walked out of the room, Maestro Ormandy advised me, "Play only first trumpet. You are a first trumpet, and you have an innate sense of playing everything musically correct." (I had to wait until I got home to ask my mother what "innate" meant!) I called him back almost five years to the day, only to hear, "I'm so sorry; I just engaged Gil Johnson from the New Orleans Symphony." *Being at the right place at the right time* really is the key.

Ormandy was right—I was a natural first trumpet and enjoyed a fifteen-year career as a principal trumpet in both symphony and opera. I always made a point of attending every rehearsal and every performance, giving 110 percent to try to make the music great. What I am most proud of, however, is that in my entire career I never had a conductor, any *conductor*, change the interpretation of any solo I ever played.

Now I had to fulfill the commitment I had made to attend college. What made my promise so difficult to keep was that most orchestral jobs were full-time positions that left no room for school. As luck would have it, a $5-a-year investment I had made with the New York Talent Agency paid enormous dividends. Musicians all over the country could hear about upcoming auditions through a unique system of communication created by two members of the New York Philharmonic: your five dollar fee ensured you would always receive a postcard notifying you of upcoming auditions. In June 1953 I received a postcard that changed my life, informing me of an audition for principal trumpet with the Tulsa Philharmonic Orchestra

Having recently auditioned for Ormandy, Szell, and Stokowski, to play for Tulsa's H. Arthur Brown—whom I'd never heard of didn' faze me. When I showed up to audition at the Barbizon Plaza Hotel ir New York, Maestro Brown apologized and told me he was sorry, bu none of the trumpet music had yet arrived. Without missing a beat, asked him, "What would you like to hear?" "Anything?" he replied in amazement. "Anything in the standard trumpet repertoire." Maestro Brown requested ten or twelve of the most famous trumpet solos, the ones that you would expect at any audition. I played Don Juan; the trumpet calls from Beethoven's Leonore overtures, Moussorsgky's "Pictures at an Exhibition," Petroushka. I was immediately offered a contract, and it was truly a dream contract, for it allowed me to fulfill my goal of learning the repertoire. But the real miracle was I was simultaneously offered the opportunity to study at the University of Tulsa and earn my bachelor of music education degree. This was only possible because Tulsa was a part-time orchestra and rehearsed in the evenings as many of its members had full-time jobs. My contract paid me $1200 for the twenty-week season, and it also included a four-year full-tuition scholarship. Later I added to my income by picking up local dance gigs.

When I got off the plane in Tulsa, Oklahoma that very hot day in September 1953, I did not know a soul. As I walked into my dormitory, it quickly became clear that I was entering an academic world with its own peculiar language. A fellow in his mid-20's sat on the couch, smoking a pipe. To my cheerful, "Hi, I'm Ronnie Modell," he replied, "You are a visceral tonic endomorph!" which completely took me aback. I didn't know whether to kiss him or punch him in the mouth! It turned out; he was a graduate student in psychology who was studying why people eat the way they do. I later found out that a visceral tonic ectomorph is someone who eats because if they didn't, they would die. A visceral tonic endomorph was someone who, when asked if they would prefer sex or food, would have to think about it.

Tulsa University turned out to be a friendly place. My dormitory, Kemp Hall, stood near the University Center, which also housed the cafeteria where we ate our meals. It had a lot of nice people working there, starting with Mrs. Hobbs, the sweet, charming lady at the information desk. Her boss, director Jess Choteau, became a great friend to me. In the cafeteria, I met Kinard, my main man who served up the food. I loved Kinard! He saw to it that I never went hungry, and with his great smile he was a joy to have in my day-to-day life on campus.

My roommate, Leonard Ramrus, was a violinist from Brooklyn. Like me, he played in the Tulsa Philharmonic while a student at TU as well. We got along great. After I pledged Pi Kappa Alpha, I moved into the frat house. We were the only frat house on sorority row, a seven-to-one Greek ratio that my frat buddies and I thoroughly enjoyed.

My first day with Tulsa's Golden Hurricane Marching Band was a shock. At James Monroe High School in the Bronx, all our marching band ever did was come out in block band formation, march down to the flag, play the National Anthem, and march off. That first day at Tulsa I was handed a ten-page chart that looked to me to be in a foreign language. We were expected to march 180 steps a minute, and asked to memorize all ten pages of complex formations. There were lots of yard-line markers, lots or R's and L's. To make matters worse, the temperature was in the nineties every day, so I was in trouble. Dwight Dailey, the new band director, had just come from the University of Michigan, which had one of the best marching band programs in the country.

I mastered the intricacies of playing with the band, and by my senior year we were a tight-knit group. In my senior year at our final marching band performance, my friends in the band decided to play an outrageous practical joke on me. We used to march out in block band for the pre-game show and then form a "T" and a "U." I was marching in the straight line that made up the "T," about half way down. As we moved from block band into the "TU," the guys in front and in back of me closed up my space, so the fans saw one lone individual, me, with a trumpet, in full uniform, running up and down the line, begging for somebody to let me in! All of this was happening at 180 steps a minute as I kept frantically trying to find some way to re-enter. I am sure it looked comical and ridiculous from the stands.

As a Jewish kid from the Bronx, there was a certain amount of culture shock I encountered living in Tulsa, Oklahoma. In my first weeks there, I met a young lady who played violin in the orchestra. We dated a few times, and after one of our concerts she introduced me to her mom and dad. They seemed to be pleasant people, and from our brief visit I could not imagine what would happen next.

I received a phone call one afternoon in my dormitory from the mother of the young lady. Her exact words to me were: "I don't want you dating my daughter anymore." Quite surprised, I asked her why. "Because," she replied, "I just found out you a Jew bastard!" I asked her what had changed from our initial meeting when she and her husband had remarked to their daughter, "What a nice young man!" At that, she hung up the phone.

After gathering myself together, I remembered that the family were members of the Christian Science Church. I instantly remembered visiting the Mary Baker Eddy home outside of Boston while I was traveling with the Cornelia Otis Skinner show--the wife of our conductor, Anne Shilkret, was a Christian Scientist who had kindly introduced me to the mother church through our visit to its founder's home. That evening I called Anne Shilkret and described the phone call to her. She was very upset, and after she called the mother church the following day, the Tulsa parents received a phone call, which left no doubt that they would not be welcomed as church members, if anything of this nature ever happened again.

That was not the last of it. When I did my student teaching senior year at Wilson Junior High School, one of my students floored me with a similar comment. The night of our concert, as I stood in the hall waiting to go on and conduct, I noticed a thirteen-year-old boy staring at me intently, one of the students whom I had worked with all semester. When I questioned why he was staring at me, he asked me, "Are you a Jew?" I said, "Yes I am," and he explained, "I ain't never seen one before." "How do I look?" I asked him, and his response was silence. My response was to put my arm around his shoulder and say, hey let's go in and make some pretty music. He was the son of a Baptist minister.

Despite incidents like these, my years at Tulsa University were wonderful. None of us ever realize at the time that college is often one of the happiest and most important periods of our lives. I had great professors at Tulsa, including my freshman year theory teacher, Getty Krieg Murphy. One of the funniest experiences in my college career took place in her class.

We were given the assignment to choose any hymn, retain the original words, and then write our own melody using the 1,4,5 chords. I really, really tried to compose an original melody, but everything ended up sounding Jewish to me—minor chords that just didn't jive with the lyrics. Finally, at midnight I went into the office of our housemother, who was a very devout Presbyterian woman. I took her Presbyterian hymnal, turned to its cleanest page (hoping nobody knew this hymn), and copied the words and music, note for note. The next day I put it on Mrs. Murphy's desk with everybody else's.

As fate would have it, I left to use the bathroom, and when I returned I found the entire class singing my "original" hymn from memory. Unfortunately, in my ignorance I had chosen the very popular "Stand Up, Stand Up for Jesus." Adding to my woes, Getty Kreig Murphy was a church organist, who knew this hymn as well as I knew the "Star Spangled Banner." I was terribly embarrassed, kept after class, and dressed down by Mrs. Murphy, who told me in no uncertain terms that all of my work had to be truly original.

I embarrassed myself again in my freshman orientation class, taught by Dr. Bela Rosza, who had been a protege of the composer Arnold Schoenberg. At the end of our first class, Dr. Rosza asked us to write a paper describing our feelings about music and what it meant to us. After he had read my paper, he asked me to stay after class. Dr. Rosza looked hard at me and said, "You're from New York City. I would expect this from someone out here, but you're from New York. How could you write such a paper?" My paper had said I had enjoyed all music with the exception of three composers Schoenberg, Alban Berg, and Anton Webern—all of whom were his idols, teachers, and heroes. New to me, however, was their use of the twelve-tone scale as an innovative form of musical writing.

I had heard that Dr. Rosza was a good chess player, and I fancied myself (an eighteen-year-old kid from the Bronx), a pretty good player as well. So I went up to him after class and suggested, "Why don't we play a game of chess for my final grade? If I win, I will choose my own grade, and if I don't, I'll accept what you give me." That was fine with Dr. Rosza. At a reception at his home for a visiting soloist, he suggested we take time out for our game.

He took me into a room where the first thing I saw was four giant chess boards set up to play. My gaze went up to a plaque over the door that read, "World's Corresponding Chess Champion, Bela Rosza, 1944-1954." He smirked at me, asking "Would you still like to play?" Being the brash young kid, I responded, "Absolutely!" It took Dr. Rosza about seven minutes to beat me. He said he would have done it in three, but I was making such idiotic moves that he thought perhaps he was seeing some new offense that he had never encountered before.

I had several classes with Dr. Rosza—Counterpoint, Orchestration, and Composition. He was brilliant man and a brilliant teacher, for those who were on his lofty level. But I think that sometimes being brilliant can get in the way of being a great teacher for the average student. Certainly below-average students won't stand a chance.

During my second year at Tulsa University, I was appointed music director of our FM radio station, KWGS, which had a wide listening audience. I was very anxious that my first live show be a big success, and I invited H. Arthur Brown, the conductor of the Tulsa Philharmonic Orchestra, as my guest.

The interview was going well, but little did I know that disaster was looming. Every radio announcer has what's known as a "panic button," to cover up a cough or to immediately go off-air. I announced that we would now hear the Tulsa Philharmonic play Tchaikovsky's Sixth Symphony, "the Pathetique." But I couldn't get the word out, repeating "the pathapoo the pathapea, the pethapa," until in desperation I hit the panic button to hide my own laughter. I was chagrined to make this mistake in front of my own conductor, but even the reserved Maestro Brown allowed himself a chuckle.

I didn't date very much in college. I was always tremendously busy, but my weight continued to be a factor, at least in my own mind. However, during my sophomore year, a lovely majorette in the marching band, Joanne Payne, invited me to join her and her folks up in their Arkansas cabin. I was eager to make a good impression, so I drew on my vast movie experience to try and emulate the great cowboys of my youth. My roommate, Charlie Locke, who hailed from Monahans, Texas, owned two beautiful pearl-handled pistols, and he loaned them to me for that weekend.

You could not drive directly to the cabin, but had to park your car and then go in on horseback. Of course, I had never ridden a horse in my life, but I did have my two guns strapped to me, just like in the movies, though the effect was marred by my suburban-style coat. I had also borrowed Charlie's ten-gallon hat: I was going to show them that this Bronx kid knew how to be a real cowboy! The horse they put me on was perfect for me. She was an old mare who would hardly move. I would only venture "Giddyup" in a hushed tone for fear the horse would bolt. At the cabin, which lacked running water, Joanne's dad said to me "Let's go out and get a rick of wood for the fireplace." I had no idea what a "rick of wood" was, thinking perhaps he meant four or five pieces. It turned out to be a lot of wood! It was freezing, and they gave me long underwear. I remember we all slept in bunk beds.

One of the biggest thrills and frights of my life came the next day when we all went horseback riding. This time I was given a young stallion to ride, who when I kicked him in the same manner I had kicked the mare, took off and started galloping, oblivious to my "Whoa horsey, whoa!" until Joanne caught up to me and managed to grab the reins and stop that animal from scaring the daylights out of me. Nonetheless, the visit was a wonderful experience, and I enjoyed Joanne and her folks immensely.

During my junior year at Tulsa, I was required to take "Educational Psychology," and my fellow students advised me that I should avoid taking it with Dr. Kirkpatrick. This, I was not able to do. We did not get off on a good note. On the first day of class, Dr. Kirkpatrick passed out a detailed syllabus and then arranged for each student to sit at least one desk away from the next student. He passed out a paper, instructing us, "Put these face down and don't turn them over until I tell you to." I looked at the guy next to me, two seats away, and said "Welcome to the Gestapo!" Dr. Kirkpatrick, it turned out, had stopped right behind me, and he leaned down and put his face to mine, asking me, "Would you like to leave now?" "No, Dr. Kirkpatrick, I signed up for the whole semester."

He was tough, but he was good, and he really knew his subject. He had very strict attendance rules, dropping you a grade for only one absence. But he showed a soft side when I approached him to let him know I would have to miss his Friday class to try to drive fifteen hundred miles non-stop to New York in an effort to see my grandmother. My mother had just called me with the sad news that she was dying. Dr. Kirkpatrick spoke to me emotionally: "Please be careful. I want to see you back here again." I came to understand that despite our exchanges, he really did like me, and I was very moved by that.

Ideally, one's worldview is expanded in College. A sociology course I took on "Marriage and the Family" opened my eyes to another aspect of the world outside my Bronx childhood. During my years at Tulsa University, there were only three Jewish students in the entire campus population. One day during class, our professor, Dr. Sandor Kovacs, looked directly at me and said, "The Jewish people are some of the most segregated people in our country." I did a double-take, thinking "Are you kidding? How can you say that? Quickly I mentally ran through all the people that my parents knew socially—and I could not come up with one Gentile. I did not think my mom or dad were prejudiced in any way. So this was an interesting idea to me. It seemed to be true. I still remember how vividly it struck me. But as I went through life, I realized that the same could be said for the Greeks, the Italians, the Poles, etc. Most people seem to be drawn to their own ethnic backgrounds.

Throughout my years at Tulsa, I was in a most unusual situation: here I was, an eighteen-year-old freshman playing first trumpet in the Tulsa Philharmonic, surrounded in the orchestra by my day-time instructors at the university. I could not have had a better conductor than Tulsa's maestro, H. Arthur Brown, and under him I had four glorious years playing principal trumpet. I learned much of the standard repertoire, for the orchestra never held back on programming.

In my first season, we played a memorable all-Gershwin program, beginning with "Strike Up the Band," followed by "Cuban Overture", and then a medley of "Porgy and Bess," arranged by Robert Russell Bennett. After intermission, we performed "Rhapsody in Blue" and "An American in Paris."

I got on the phone after our first rehearsal and called my uncle Louis, still the principal trumpet of the Cleveland Orchestra, moaning to him that I didn't have the chops to get through a program like this, particularly because we had only three trumpets; there was no fourth, no assistant. He laughed and laughed until I said, "What's so funny?" "Welcome to the club, my boy!" he replied. "Now listen to me and I'll tell you how to get through this kind of program without an assistant."

Uncle Louis gave me simple, good advice. Look for the unisons where all the trumpets are playing the same notes, lay out, and save yourself for the big exposed solos. If the conductor gives you flak during the dress rehearsal for not putting out all that you should, ask him simply if he wants to hear it now, or if he wants to hear it at the concert. This is a standard line with all players. Learning how to pace oneself to get through, was a valuable lesson. I came to learn that sections that work together, stay together, and play together, always seem to be successful. Not only did I get through the program, but had bloody chops at what was to be one of my more memorable concerts.

In the spring of 1954, I fell in love with opera. Playing with the Tulsa Opera Company gave me my first experience playing it, and opera became the love of my life. If I was stranded on a desert island and given the choice of the music I wanted to hear for all eternity, I would choose to listen to Puccini operas.

That spring the Tulsa Philharmonic performed the concert version of "Tosca," starring Toscanini's favorite soprano, Herva Nelli, with the well-known baritone Robert Weede as Scarpia.

In a live performance, anything can happen. The cast had been instructed to learn their roles in English, in these days before subtitles were provided. Then one week before the concert, Herva Nelli arrived unable to speak one word of English. This was a disaster, and it created havoc with the cast. Switching back and forth between Italian and

English caused enormous confusion. Nelli was given a tutor and finally got to the point where she could sing most of the opera in English, except for her great aria in the second act, "Vis d'arte," which she adamantly refused to sing in this new language.

At our concert, after all kinds of mis-cues, the great scene between Tosca and Scarpia began to unfold, in which Scarpia has Tosca's lover, Cavaradossi, tortured as she listens. Scarpia makes a deal with Tosca: if she will sleep with him, he will write an order for a fake execution, and after that the lovers can escape.

But the order he writes is instead an order to kill Cavaradossi, and as Scarpia approaches her, she picks up a letter opener and stabs him, exclaiming dramatically, "This is for all of Rome!" As she utters the line, Scarpia finally drops after a tremendous elaborate death scene. Imagine being in the audience as Tosca turns and delivers her next line, in English, with a very strong New York Italian accent: "He's a-dead!" The audience was in hysterics.

The best was yet to come. At the opera's conclusion, realizing her lover is dead, Tosca runs to the top of the castle and prepares to jump to her death. They had stacked a bunch of mattresses behind the castle and instructed Herva Nelli to land on her knees to stop herself and kill the fall. At that point, the orchestra, lead by the trumpet, comes in with the famous theme "E lucevan le stelle." I always tried to memorize my trumpet parts so that I would be able to watch the action, but this was one time I was sorry I had done that. As Herva Nelli delivered her final lines, and jumped, she forgot to land on her knees. Landing feet first, she bounced up to where the audience could actually see her entire body suspended in the air before dropping to the mattress again. Of course, it was enormously funny, and I messed up every note of that beautiful theme. I know that Maestro Brown was not happy with me, but there was no way I could stay in control after that performance.

In the spring of 1957, we were scheduled to perform Verdi's "A Masked Ball." We performed two operas each year, one in the fall and one in the spring, often with well-known guest conductors. When our conductor arrived, you could tell from the moment he walked in that he would rather have been anywhere else in the world but Tulsa, Oklahoma. He took a straight-back chair and turned it around, leaning on the front part of it. Using a pencil as a baton, he proceeded to indifferently conduct the first rehearsal. "A Masked Ball," by the way, is not an easy opera.

Imagine our shock when the following day's headline in the Tulsa newspaper announced that the Maestro had left because the orchestra was not, in his opinion, "competent enough to play the score." In the time I had been there, we had already performed "La Boheme," "Aida," "Carmen," "Madame Butterfly," "The Bartered Bride," and "Tosca." Believe me, the orchestra was very competent. What I later learned was that the Maestro had been offered the opportunity to record an opera for RCA with a major cast. Rather than explain his dilemma to the Tulsa Opera Company, perhaps with the promise of returning in the future at a reduced fee, he chose to slander the orchestra and not honor his commitments. Now suddenly, days before the opening, we had no conductor.

The next day they flew in a New York conductor, Carlo Moresco, and at the first rehearsal, it was obvious that he did not speak English. Our orchestra was composed of 80% Okies and 20% transplants from big cities, usually the principal players, such as myself. Early in the rehearsal, Maestro Moresco looked at the French horn players and told them, "Con tutta forza." Incomprehension. I leaned forward and said, "He wants a lot more power, a lot more force." He said something else to the bassoons and I whispered his message to them. At our break, the maestro called me up to the podium: "Prima tromba. Parla Italiano?" "Un poco," I replied. He made me understand that if I would act as his interpreter, he would ask the orchestra to add an extra $50 to my paycheck.

For the next three days of our rehearsals, every time we reached a particular spot, our conductor would look at the trombones, put his hands straight out, and cry "Basta! Basta! Tromboni, basta," meaning "enough!" or "too loud!" At our dress rehearsal, everyone was nervous because we hadn't had enough time to rehearse. When we reached that spot, the maestro freaked out. He used every Italian cuss word I had ever heard and ended his tirade by looking at the two trombone players and bellowing, "Prima donna mi coglioni!" Translation: "You are the prima donna of my balls!"

Instantly, Bill McPeters, one of the trombonists sitting behind me, poked me with his trombone slide. He said to me, The Interpreter, "If he said what I think he said, I'm a-gonna bust 'im in the mouth! What'd he say?" I simply replied, "Too loud." McPeters said, "You mean, alla that mumbo jumbo was jus 'too loud'?" "Well yes," I told him, "he has a very fancy way of saying it, but the essence of it is, too loud." So we avoided a fist-fight in the pit. I returned to New York the following year, but I heard later from a friend that the following season, during an actual performance, Maestro Moresco got into a fist-fight with the principal bass player, Herman Burkhardt. Italian opera people feel the three most important things in the world are opera, God, and country, like Texans whose lives revolve around football, God, and country

The last opera that I played in Tulsa was Verdi's "Il Trovatore," starring two of opera's legends, singing at the end of their careers. What an honor it was to finish my time at Tulsa working with the great Swedish tenor Jussi Bjoerling and the great baritone Leonard Warren.

During one of our first rehearsals, our principal clarinetist Dwight Dailey, also Tulsa University's marching band director, was smoking his pipe in the pit and the smoke apparently wafted up toward the stage. Jussi Bjoerling walked up to the front of the stage, looked at our conductor, and announced, "Maestro! I will not sing another note while this smoke comes up from the pit." Bjoerling was wearing an elegant camel hair coat. As he walked away, one of our percussionists looked at the conductor and asked in a broad Oklahoma twang, "Maestro, would you tell that tenor to observe the mistletoe on my coattail?" Of course, this was a disrespectful thing to say to one of the greatest tenors in the world, but I don't think he knew who Jussi Bjoerling was!.

When we performed "Madama Butterfly," one of my very favorite operas, our production starred the renowned soprano Dorothy Kirsten. Miss Kirsten had not married until late in life, and her tragic story was that her marriage was a great love affair cut short when her husband suddenly fell ill and died. She had stopped singing for a number of years. This was the first opera she performed after coming out of her grief--an absolutely magnificent performance.

Following our opening night, there was a big ball at Tulsa's Mayo Hotel. Knowing the story of how Ms. Kirsten had lost her husband, seeing her sitting there dressed so elegantly and beautifully, quite alone, struck me as very sad. I simply went over to her and asked, "Would you like to dance?" So I took Dorothy Kirsten out on the dance floor. As my beautiful wife Kathy can tell you, I don't really dance. I can slow dance, but I don't even do that very well. Whatever they were playing, I am sure it was a slow number or I never would have had the courage to ask Miss Kirsten to dance. It was a wonderful moment and a great thrill for a twenty-two-year-old young man from the Bronx to dance with this opera diva. I felt really lucky.

In May of 1957, I had accomplished a major goal: receiving my bachelor of music education degree from the University of Tulsa, as well as gaining four years of invaluable experience learning the symphonic repertoire. My ultimate goal, however, was to land a spot in one of the top five orchestras, and with that in mind, I moved back to New York City after graduation, where all the auditions for major orchestras were held. Like many young people today, I moved back in with my parents in their small West Bronx apartment. To make ends meet, I played that summer at the Catskills' Pines Hotel, and of course, my connection to Joe Cuba there, led me into the world of Latin music.

Late that fall, I received a call from my Uncle Milty with the news that he needed surgery on his middle finger and would need a replacement for his position as principal trumpet in the New Jersey Symphony. I filled in for him for about two months, and between this and my Latin gigs I was just making enough to survive. Auditions were proving to be scarce.

In January of 1958, the principal harpist in the Chicago Symphony called me and asked if I would play an audition for his close friend Maestro Vladimir Golschmann. Formerly the conductor of the St. Louis Symphony, Maestro Golschmann had just accepted the position of musical director of the Tulsa Philharmonic. After auditioning a his apartment in New York City, Golschmann quickly made me an incredible offer: at double my previous salary, I would play principal trumpet and also receive a full scholarship at Tulsa University, this time to earn my master's degree in music performance.

After my first season back at Tulsa, I spent the following summer playing a twelve-week season at the North Shore Theater in Beverly, Massachusetts. In August my father, still driving a cab in New York City, phoned me with the startling news that the great maestro Leopold Stokowski had just ridden in his cab and was curious about what I was doing. My dad had driven Stokowski on other occasions, and the maestro was familiar with both me and my uncle Louis Davidson. Stokowski inquired, "Well, why don't you have your son call me? There will be an opening for principal trumpet in the Houston Symphony next season. I would really like to hear him play." I was shocked that he remembered my playing from our 1953 audition (during my Cornelia Otis Skinner tour). When I called Stokowki, we arranged to meet at noon on September 4, 1959 at his luxurious apartment overlooking Central Park.

I got on the elevator in his building, and when it opened up I found I was right in his apartment, a new experience for me. And there he was, in an elegant robe and ascot, the kind you see in the movies, tall and imposing, with his hair sticking straight up. Sitting nearby was one of the most beautiful women I had ever seen. Stokowki suggested I take out my horn and warm up, and I went into the next room so as not to be distracted.

A significant detail for this story is that Stokowski was then enduring a bitter and nasty divorce from Gloria Vanderbilt. After I played for the maestro, he sat at his desk, with his back to me, and filled out an information card with my particulars. He asked me, "What is your current address?" I gave it to him. "What is your current telephone number?" I gave that too. Then he queried, "You are married?" "No, Maestro," I replied, "but as a matter of fact, I am getting married this Monday afternoon." Without looking up, lifting his head, or turning around, he responded tonelessly in an affected European accent, "You are in for a lot of trouble." He paused, and then moved on to the next question. I have never forgotten the way he expressed his feelings!

Stokowski offered me the job at Houston, but when he discovered that I was under contract at Tulsa with his good friend Vladimir Golschmann, he told me, "Golschmann is my friend, and I cannot ask you to jump your contract to come to Houston."

When I returned to Tulsa, I had the pleasure of working for Maestro Golschmann. What a charming man and what a delight to play for! He had spent twenty-seven years with the St Louis Symphony and had conducted the Cleveland Orchestra when Erich Leinsdorf was drafted into the Army in the middle of the season. He was always the consummate professional, trying to get the best out of the orchestra. Golschmann was wonderful to work with; never a cross moment in any of our rehearsals.

Something changed, however, during the week prior to the arrival in Tulsa of the great pianist Artur Rubenstein, who with Vladimir Horowitz was at the time one of the two giants of the keyboard. After we played an overture, Rubenstein was to perform a Chopin concerto in the first half of the program. Following intermission, he would play the famous Tchaikovsky Concerto Number One in B-flat. All of a sudden, during the week of rehearsal, Golschmann was not himself. He was irritable and irascible, not at all like the person we knew. What I discovered was that Artur Rubenstein was his close, good friend—they were like brothers—and Golschmann wanted the best possible orchestral accompaniment for his dear friend. So he was snapping at everything and everyone.

In the last moment of the Tchaikovsky concerto, due to its complex rhythmic patterns, it is extremely challenging for the orchestra to stay with the soloist and vice versa. At our dress rehearsal, we got through the Tchaikovsky concerto and it went well, so we were feeling as if a two thousand-pound weight had been taken off our shoulders. As the last note sounded and Golschmann cut off the orchestra, our timpanist Chuck Featherstone, a dyed-in-the-wool Okie, raised his hand and asked, in his broad Oklahoma drawl, "Maestro, seven bars from the end am I supposed to be forte or mezzo forte?" Golschmann looked at him and replied, in his French-tinged accent, "That should be *mein egine tsuras!*" (Translation from the Yiddish: "That should be my only worry!") Ninety-nine percent of the orchestra had no idea what he just said, but Artur Rubenstein and I burst out laughing. What a delightful memory of this great artist and great conductor!

During the 1959 season at Tulsa, I was invited to audition for the principal trumpet chair in the Minneapolis Symphony Orchestra, an opportunity that would have brought me closer to my ultimate goal. According to the letter I received afterwards from Bernard Adelstein, the principal trumpet player, I had played an "excellent audition" and according to the current conductor, Antal Dorati, "If I were staying on in Minneapolis, Ronnie would have the job." The final decision, Bernie wrote, came down to the other finalist having a two-week longer season, hence more experience than I had. It is so ironic that this experience had a profound impact on my life and career: if I had landed this position, I probably would never have been involved with jazz education

RONNIE AND SANDY - AGES 1 AND 4

MOM AND POP - MY LAST YEAR IN DALLAS 1969

milton, Louie & David Davidson

MILTY, LOUIS AND GRANDPA DAVIDSON
THREE OF MY HEROES

POP AND RON - THE SWEETEST MAN I EVER MET

LANCE, RON, SANDY
MY BROTHERS, 2 OF THE GREATEST CONTRIBUTORS
TO MAKING THE WORLD A BETTER PLACE

**MY FIRST BAND - ME ON THE EXTREME LEFT,
STEIRS HOTEL 1950**

**SCOTT AND CORNELIA OTIS SKINNER
MY SON SCOTT 6 MONTHS OLD HAS A NEW NECLKACE**

22 YRS., FROM **9** & **10** YR. OLDS
TO COLLEGE & SEMI-PRO

PBS SPECIAL 1969
FOR KIDS 3-5, MY DAUGHTER LISA MARIE IN THE MIDDLE

LUNCHEON I GAVE FOR THE **CSO** BRASS & ALL **NIU**
BRASS MAJORS. THINK "BUD" LIKED MY JOKE.

ME AND DOC CHEATHAM

MARIO BAUZA AND MACHITO TRUMPET SECTION.
N.Y. PALLADADIUM, 1958

**BOBBY TUCKER, DEAR FRIEND, MENTOR, PIANIST
ARRANGER FOR BILLIE HOLIDAY & BILLY ECKSTIN**

"JAKE" DON JACOBY, ONE OF A KIND, BELOVED BY ALL

KATHY AND RON WITH THE LOUIS AND CLARK EXPEDITION

"CAT" ANDERSON AT ITG PARTY,
WITH BOB GIARDINELLI & CHARLIE SCHLEUTER

DUKE ELLINGTON, THE NIGHT OF HIS LAST CONCERT AT NIU
MOST ELEGANT MAN I EVER MET

"POPS", LOUIS ARMSTRONG AND ME,
1966 AT THE PINES HOTEL IN THE CATSKILLS

DIZZY GILLESPIE, ON TOUR WITH NIU JAZZ ENS. WARMING UP

JAMES MOODY, DIZZY CALLED HIM ONE OF THE TOP SAXOPHONISTS OF HIS TIME

**LOUIS BELLSON AND WIFE PEARL
RECEIVING DOCTORATE AT NIU**

STAN KENTON - GIVING CLINICS AT NIU

DALLAS: MUSICAL THRILLS BEYOND BELIEF

During the 1959-60 season, the Dallas Symphony came through Tulsa on its tour. After the concert, its conductor, Maestro Paul Kletzki, tried to contact me, with the news that he would like me to come to Dallas and audition.

When Tulsa's season ended, I traveled to Dallas to audition at the back of the State Fair Music Hall, in a ballet room cluttered with mirrors and poles. I came out to face the principal players of the Dallas Symphony: Willard Elliot (principal bassoon), Gladys Elliot (principal oboe), Leonard Posner (the concert-master), Artie Lewis (principal trombonist), and Clyde Miller (principal horn). In April 1960, it was not yet customary for auditions to played behind a screen. I was free to choose ten or twelve excerpts from the standard repertoire. Kletzki, shrugged his shoulders when I finished because I had played everything. He came up to the music stand and opened up the music to the "Infernal Dance" in Stravinsky's "Firebird," which I zipped through. But then he had me play the third movement from Bruckner's seventh symphony, in F-trumpet so I had to transpose. Unfortunately, at the time I only owned a B-flat trumpet. The music was a scherzo with accidentals all over the place (sharps and flats), and I was so overwhelmed I had to stop several times. Kletzki looked at me and asked, "How long would it take you to learn this?" My response was, "Probably two days of serious wood-shedding." The next day I got the call offering me a contract with the Dallas symphony, a twenty-five week season for the grand salary of $4000. But what was I going to do for the other twenty-seven weeks? I was already married with a small child.

I got to spend only one season with Kletzki, but it was absolutely marvelous. I just adored this man—everything from his facial expressions to his incredible knowledge of Brahms and Mahler. We had fun that season with "Dance of Vengeance" from Samuel Barber's "Medea." At one place in the score, it shifted from a 3/4 bar to a 5/8 bar, meaning there were three beats in one bar and 5 beats in the next. In each rehearsal, Kletzki would approach it differently, and it was plain he had not yet made a decision about how he wanted to conduct it. After we played through it at our dress rehearsal, he looked at us and said

"Any questions?" I raised my hand to ask, "Maestro, when we get to this section, how will you be conducting it?" We all had a good laugh when he responded, "I knew I shouldn't have hired you!" But I did force his decision, for he added, "Definitely 3 beats and 5 beats," and we played it beautifully at our concert. It was such a shame that Dallas music critic John Rosenfield maligned Kletzki with his scathing reviews and forced his resignation at the end of that season. Rosenfield had torn apart Kletzki's performances of Brahms, a composer that Kletzki held sacred. I was extremely fortunate to have spent one season with him.

In our three-week tour that year, we finished every night with "Brahms third symphony," which ends with an F-major chord, the trumpet on top playing the highest note of the chord pianissimo. For the first six nights, I tried to attack that last chord, that concert F—but again, there I was with my B-flat trumpet. I would either "put hair on the note" (musicians term for a non clean attack), or I would crack it, or it wouldn't come out at all. On the fourth day in Iowa, I walked into an elevator and encountered Kletzki.

I looked at him and simply said, "Maestro, I am so sorry." Every night I had played every note perfectly except for that one note that I was repeatedly missing. Kletzki said nothing, just gave me a little love tap across the cheek and a smile, and I suddenly realized that he wanted that note to sound like a flower opening in slow motion. He did not want to hear any attack whatsoever.

The Brahms symphony has only two trumpet parts. Our third trumpet was a wonderful old Italian man, Joe Cinquemanni. The night we played at Iowa State University in Ames, I asked him to come out and sit through the entire symphony. "I just need you," I told him, "to play one or two bars toward the end and let me rest and get set for that last chord." It worked: that night it came out just the way Kletzki had envisioned it. When I played that last note, clean and beautiful as an opening flower, the entire orchestra applauded, turned around, and made the traditional orchestral gesture of acclaim—they shuffled their feet. I never missed the note after that.

After Kletzki's departure, Donald Johanos was appointed conductor. Our good fortune was that Georg Solti had left the Los Angeles Philharmonic and was available for part of that 1961-1962 season.

Given Solti's reputation, we were all both excited and apprehensive. At his first concert, the orchestra performed Beethoven's "Egmont Overture," the suite from Stravinsky's "Petroushka," and the "Brahms First Symphony." This was his way of testing us because the program was very challenging in many areas. Solti and I hit it off great, and in our first ten concerts he gave me six solo bows, including one after "Petroushka." His repertoire included many difficult trumpet parts. I remember one concert when "Bach's Third Suite" for D-Trumpet was followed by Hindemith's "Mathis der Mahler," a very difficult night for me because I never had great endurance. The next concert featured Bartok's "Miraculous Mandarin," "Till Eulenspiegel," a Beethoven piano concerto, and concluded with Debussy's "La Mer." Finally, by the fifth week, we were playing "Schumann's Fourth Symphony," which gave me some relief.

Solti had the greatest rehearsal technique that I have ever encountered. His way was to come in, play through a movement of something, and then have you put your instrument in your lap. He would then discuss the changes he wanted to make. It was very different from Kletzki, who was always laid back until the middle of the week, when he would start to become more and more nervous. By the following Monday at our dress rehearsal, we always expected to work overtime, because by then Kletzki would start to panic.

Solti was the complete opposite. He came in like a human dynamo, and he stayed a dynamo for the entire week. When I told him he was the only conductor I'd ever met with this rehearsal technique, he answered, "Look. If we do our work the way we should, when it's time for the concert we should all be able to relax and enjoy the work that we have accomplished." What a great theory and a great way to rehearse! Solti made things easy, not difficult. The most dynamic thing about him was the excitement in his eyes when he conducted.

In contrast to Solti's wonderful rehearsal technique, his successor Donald Johanos would "stop and pick," constantly interrupting the flow of the music. It is always interesting to observe the different styles of conductors. For instance, Solti never called anybody by their name; it was always "first trumpet," or "second clarinet." Kletzki, however, always knew not only every musician's name, but the names of their wives and children.

Solti and I would meet occasionally in his dressing room, where we would discuss specifics on how he wanted the brass section to perform. When he left to guest-conduct the New York Philharmonic, I brought him a photo and asked him to autograph it for me. Solti was looking down at his desk, took a pen, never looked up, and asked me, "What is your name?" I was so completely floored that I took the picture home and couldn't look at it for twenty-four hours. When I finally did, he had inscribed, "To Ronald Modell, the excellent first trumpet of the Dallas Symphony, my best wishes for your continued success."

I was extremely honored when Solti accepted the invitation I extended to him to my home for lunch. He instructed me, "No fish, no fowl." Being from Budapest, I made him Hungarian stuffed cabbage, and he loved it. That afternoon I played a recording for him that he had never heard—the classic 1928 recording of the New York Philharmonic doing "Ein Heldenleben" with William Mengelberg conducting and he loved that, too.

By the second half of the season, however, everybody thought Solti was out of his mind. He scheduled an extremely challenging Stravinsky program with only eleven hours of rehearsal time. The orchestra had never played "Stravinsky's Symphony in Three Movements," which is every bit as difficult as "The Rite of Spring." We also performed the "Symphony of Psalms" with the University of North Texas choir. We concluded with "*The Rite of Spring*," which the orchestra hadn't played in fifteen years.

We started rehearsing "*The Rite*" on the first day, and when we got to the last three pages, where every bar has a different meter, people started coming in at the wrong place, and it soon became ridiculous.

To calm everyone down, Solti stopped the orchestra, and in a comedic way, told us, "Look, from now on, whoever comes in wrong has to donate twenty-five cents, and at the end of the week we will take the money and throw ourselves a party." Everyone laughed, which lightened the mood, and by the time of the concert we were playing Stravinsky beautifully. I happened to notice as I was leaving after the first performance of the Stravinsky, that Solti's dressing room door was open. I looked in and asked him, "Maestro, how did you do with the money this week?" He looked at me and said, "We'll call it even." Later I was very surprised to learn that this had been the first time Solti had ever conducted "The Rite of Spring." Playing with a conductor of his stature and talent was a priceless experience for the orchestra.

Many people have asked me, "How really important is the conductor? You guys are the ones playing, and he just looks like he's waving his arms up there." The best way I can describe Solti is that he made the Dallas Symphony believe that it was the Chicago Symphony, considered one of the five best orchestras in the world. He possessed that kind of power. He inspired the orchestra to play at a level where it had never played before.

After Solti left, Donald Johanos assumed the full conductorship in the 1962-63 season. He was a good conductor; there were certain things he did well, and like most conductors, there were certain things he should have avoided in the repertoire. Everything went well the first five or six years with the orchestra and Johanos, until the orchestra made its first-ever appearance at Carnegie Hall.

We were on a long, six-week tour, and in New York we were set to premiere Gunther Schuller's new symphony. It was commissioned by the Dallas Public Library for the Carnegie Hall concert. Schuller came to Dallas a few days before we started the tour, and he was still writing the piece while we were in rehearsal. It was a very challenging piece of music, especially the last movement, which was written in the style of Bach's Brandenburg concerti, featuring oboe, flute, and D-trumpet.

Because the Dallas Symphony was so highly regarded, six major critics attended our concert at Carnegie Hall. Four of them gave us glowing reviews, perhaps even more glowing than we deserved, thanks to some Dallas backers who made sure of it. Critic Miles Kastendick, however, gave us a scathing and unfair review. We received our most honest critique from Harold Schoenberg of the New York Times, who pronounced us one of the top twenty orchestras in the world, with excellent first-chair players.

But I must tell you that during our performance of "Schuller's First Symphony," there were people in the balcony hissing and waving handkerchiefs. The music was very avant garde. After the concert, when we adjourned to the famous Carnegie Tavern for a drink, I sat at the table with my mom, dad, and Uncle Milty. When I asked Gertie how she had like the Schuller piece, she confessed, "Well, it wasn't exactly my cup of tea, because it had all of these . . . (making sound effects) . . . beep beep aaawww eeee aawww eee…"

When I came off stage after performing Schuller's piece, I knew I had played it well. Gunther Schuller was there to praise me and give me a big hug. But Johanos was *also* standing there, turned his back and walked away, which I thought was strange. From that point on, and for the rest of the tour, Johanos's demeanor on the podium changed. All intelligent conductors know that when they have good first-chair players, they simply let them play. There is nothing wrong, of course, with a conductor offering his interpretation of how a solo should be played. But with the heady reviews, Johanos now seemed determined to intervene. After we left New York, we could do no right. He was going to show us how to do it.

By the time we played in Johnston, Pennsylvania, the entire brass section came up to me, its unofficial concertmaster, and told me in no uncertain terms that I had better go to Johanos and tell him he had to stop putting his hand up all the time. Shushing the brass section was something he had never done before prior to New York. When we were performing Richard Strauss's "Der Rosenkavalier," Johanos was suddenly finding it much too loud, making faces to indicate he was disturbed by our playing.

At intermission, I went to see him. He had been given a terrible place for his dressing room—so small, that when I went in to talk with him, we were standing belly-to-belly in our white ties and tails. There was a commode just past him, and a mirror. Just as I was about to tell him how unhappy the brass section was, a guy wearing only an undershirt and pants walked into the room without knocking, probably the building's janitor. Without an "excuse me," he walked between us, unzipped his fly, and started to pee.

It was as if somebody had taken a giant pin and stuck it in Johanos's big balloon of an ego. The guy finished what he was doing, zipped up, walked between us, and left. You could see the steam coming out of Johanos's ears: how dare someone behave this way to Donald Johanos! In a very firm voice, he asked me sharply, "What was it you wanted?" "Nothing, Don, nothing," I replied. I walked out trying with all my might not to laugh until I got back to the brass section, where I told them the story and said, "I think we may have had our problem solved tonight."

After this difficult six-week tour, we were all extremely tired when we got back to Dallas. We had only one day off before we started rehearsing Howard Hanson's "Romantic Symphony," a piece I had never played before, with Hanson himself at our rehearsals. When Johanos became conductor, he had hired many musicians from his alma mater, the Eastman School of Music.

I can honestly say that in my fifteen years of playing in symphony orchestras, I never, ever talked back to a conductor. If I had had something to say, I would have gone to his dressing room and had it out privately.

When we started our rehearsal, I noticed my part said simply "Trumpet." I think because of the difficulty of the tour and my feeling so tired, I didn't realize this was in C-trumpet, so I started playing my usual B-flat trumpet, as Johanos became more and more annoyed. Finally, he stopped the rehearsal to ask me, "What are you doing?" "It doesn't tell me what key," I told him, so I thought it was trumpet in B-flat." "It' trumpet in C!" he snapped back. His tone of voice prompted me to say in front of the orchestra and Howard Hanson, "Well, I didn't know that because I didn't go to Eastman!" Johanos immediately called for an intermission and stormed offstage. He came back twenty minutes later. I think we all realized that we were tired, and our nerves were frayed. These things happen over the course of a career. I know a lot of worse stories about bickering between conductors and principal players. I simply tried every single day of my professional life, to go in and do the best job I could. And to always be very serious at rehearsals.

I couldn't resist, however, having some fun with our very fine second trumpeter who was a notorious homophobe. Mac was a good-looking man and a muscle-builder, always in shape. He had a problem with anyone even uttering the word "queer" (nobody was saying "gay" in those days) and would freak out—"Don't talk about that! I don't want to hear about it!" I couldn't resist.

We were rehearsing the "1812 Overture," in the middle of the Cotton Bowl, and there was a section where the first trumpet had a solo, then some rest, and then the solo again. After I played the solo the first time, I leaned over close to Mac and informed him, "Mac, I found out today that there is a queer in the brass section!" before playing my solo again. He looked absolutely repulsed, and putting his face close to mine, asked me, "Who?!" I responded by kissing him on the cheek, and I really thought he was going to kill me. He eventually forgave me, but for a couple of days he wouldn't speak to me.

There were always players who didn't like conductors, but no one ever made the point more vividly than our principal oboist, Gladys Elliot. Gladys was a magnificent musician, and she loathed conductors. I had told her and the entire orchestra a joke about a small town that had a "Man on the Street" standing downtown to stop people and interview them on the radio. One morning, with no one else around to interview, the guy stopped the town drunk and asked him, "Would you like to be on the radio?" "Yeahhh, I sure woooould...." The Man on the Street said, "I like to start my interviews by asking if you know any knock-knock jokes." "Yeeeaahh," the drunk responded, "I sshhuure doooo." "Go ahead!" Drunk: "Knoooock knoooock!" Man: "Who's there?" Drunk: "Aaargo." Man: "Argo who?" Drunk: "Aaarrgooo fuck yourself!"

You will understand why I'm telling you this joke after I tell you about the week the orchestra suffered with a very mediocre conductor with an unfamiliar rehearsal technique. After several rehearsals, Gladys Elliot could no longer restrain herself. She reached into her oboe case and took out an enormous box of the world's most famous corn starch emblazoned with the name "ARGO." Gladys pointed the box right at the podium as the entire orchestra began laughing while the conductor was clueless. But that was how Gladys felt! Mission accomplished!

In the fall of 1960, after my first few weeks in the orchestra, some guys in the brass section warned me to be wary of a woman in the violin section because she was, in essence, a nymphomaniac who liked to try out every new man in the orchestra. I was certainly curious to see who this woman was.

It turned out that we became the best of friends. She shall remain nameless for as my mother taught me, unless you see something with your own eyes, don't believe anything anyone tells you. We were such great friends that when I woke up in the hospital after back surgery, the two people at my bedside were my wife and my friend. I had given myself a post-hypnotic suggestion, to have my first words on coming out of anesthesia be, "Is it a girl or a boy?" It worked! To this day, this woman and I are still friends, reconnecting last year after a lapse of twenty years.

Whenever we toured, our hotel rooms were assigned in alphabetical order, which usually placed my friend next door to me. I want you now to imagine yourself as a juror in an adultery trial. This is exactly what happened, and I wonder how you would have voted.

On the last day of our tour, we were in Big Spring, Texas, the town where they filmed "The Last Picture Show." After our concert, knowing we were leaving early the next day, I requested a wake-up call for 6:30 and in the morning promptly called the coffee shop to send up orange juice, coffee, a sweet roll, and a newspaper. The young man who knocked on my door, however, had brought up two orange juices, two coffees, two Danishes, and two newspapers. Although I explained the mistake to him, he told me to take it and that I would be only charged for one.

So I picked up my phone and called my friend, telling her of the extra breakfast and inviting her to join me. She came by; we ate and chatted, and after breakfast she opened the door of my room and stepped out into the hallway in her robe that exposed her beautiful silken nightgown. At that precise moment, the squarest guy in the entire orchestra came down the hall. My friend just smiled, looked back into my room, and said clearly, "Thanks, Ron, it was great!" So, if you are on the jury, how do you vote? I'm a dead man!

During my nine years as principal trumpet with the Dallas Symphony, I almost never missed a performance or a rehearsal. In 1967, we were scheduled to perform "Bach's Mass in B minor," one of the most challenging pieces in the trumpet repertoire. At that time, I didn't own a piccolo trumpet, which made it even more formidable. The week before the performance I began to feel ill, and my condition worsened with each passing day. After our dress rehearsal on the day of the performance, I was as sick as I had ever been. Our conductor, Johanos, was so alarmed he drove me in his own car to Baylor Hospital. After examining me, the doctor said, "This man is near pneumonia; I can hardly see his lungs. Forget about tonight, or tomorrow—he certainly is not going to play tomorrow's concert at Texas A & M."

This is not what I wanted to hear. So I insisted on playing that night, and miraculously played well. But by the next afternoon, I had broken down completely, and I just didn't have it. I had blown everything on Saturday night in Dallas—and that was the place to do it.

The very last concert I ever played with the Dallas Symphony, in 1969, was a tour concert in Shreveport, Louisiana featuring Eileen Farrell, star soprano of New York's Metropolitan Opera, in an all-Wagner program. Just before intermission, Miss Farrell sang the "Prelude and Love-Death" from "Tristan and Isolde," which she performed magnificently. As she and our conductor, Donald Johanos, were walking arm-in-arm off the stage, I saw him say something to her that drew her instant response, sending the first violin players into convulsions. I asked Peggy Miller, one of the first violinists, "What was that all about?" Apparently as they exited, smiling, to thunderous applause, Maestro Johanos said to her, "How was the tempo, my dear?" and Miss Farrell told him, "Too fucking slow!"

That was the great Eileen Farrell. Whenever she came to town, she always called me after the first rehearsal to invite me to stop by her dressing room. "Ronnie," she would say, "tell me your best dirty jokes." She was a marvelous person to be with, and *what a voice!* An interesting coincidence is that she ended her career teaching at Indiana University with her studio next to that of my uncle, Louis Davidson.

In 1964, I first branched into music education when Southern Methodist University engaged me as an adjunct professor of trumpet. In addition to my teaching responsibilities, I initiated three new programs: a stage band, a student brass ensemble, and a faculty brass quintet. There had never been a stage band before at SMU. The faculty quintet gave clinic concerts at area high schools, which served as a great recruiting tool, a technique I would use as well at NIU.

SMU was a wonderful music school. What I remember most vividly is the enthusiastic students I had there. But what was most exciting and thrilling, probably the best experience in my five years of teaching there, was serving as an associate director of the SMU Mustang Band, a marching band known as "96 Guys and a Girl." Jack Rohr, the band's writer, was one of the very first arrangers to write pieces for marching bands in a jazz style. The kids had 14 uniform changes, and in the beginning of football season the heat was so brutal that they wore Bermuda shorts and derby hats.

It was exciting to work for Irving Dreilbrodt, head of the Mustang Band, because he always surrounded himself with terrific people. I handled the trumpets and trombones. Dreilbrodt was extraordinary at motivating the students. As a freshman, if you made the band, you wore a red-and-blue "SMU Mustang Band" beanie for the year, and every kid that wore that felt as much pride as if they had been chosen to be first-string quarterback on the football team. The word "pride" was absolutely central to Dreilbrodt's success. We all were proud to be a part of the band.

Anybody who knows anything about Texas knows it's football, God, and country there, in that order. Irving Dreibrodt was magnificent at getting those kids fired up and walking out on that football field with their heads held high. He also came up with a great innovation for our marching band—having the twenty-four trumpet players all play the Dizzy Gillespie-type trumpet, so they could look down at their music while their bells were always facing up toward the stands.

A legendary story about Irving Dreibrodt came out of the Texas Music Educators Conference in San Antonio, which often drew as many as twenty thousand educators from all over the country, including the world-renowned marching band and concert band director William Revelli. Revelli was almost a god-like creature in the eyes of many people. But others saw him as a monster for the way he treated students, often bringing them to tears with his unorthodox manner of rehearsing.

One year of the conference, as Dreibrodt waited for the elevator, it opened up, and there came Revelli with an entourage of students looking up at him in total awe. Dreibrodt, who was two-thousand percent Texan and loved doing things like this, looked at him and exclaimed in a very loud voice, "Weeelll, if it ain't my old friend Ravioli!" Of course, everyone turned white. Who would dare address the great William Revelli in this disrespectful manner? But that was Dreilbrodt's way.

Dreilbrodt's remark to Revelli is a classic example of something all of us wish we had the nerve to do. My dear friend in Dallas, Harvey Anderson, a character like no other, was known for doing just that. He was also known for being notoriously late to gigs. One night, late to a gig and traveling at high speed, he was stopped by a "County Mountie," a policeman in brimmed hat, knickers, and boots. As the policeman approached his car, Harvey rolled down his window and told the officer in his great Texas drawl, "I'll have a hamburger, fries, and a chocolate shake, if you don't mind." I don't think the policeman laughed, because Harvey said he got the ticket, but what a great line. Another time, late to a concert for inmates at a Texas prison, the guard at the gate looked into his car and asked him, "Any drugs or alcohol?" Harvey replied, "Just enuff for maself!" What does it take to be able to say something like that!

My years at SMU were absolutely crucial in my development as a music educator. I wasn't aware of it at the time, but the ensembles and programs I created there gave me tremendous experience and knowledge. I would later draw upon this when I began my career at Northern Illinois University.

MAKING A BABY: CREATING JAZZ AT NIU

I first heard of Northern Illinois University during the 1967-68 Dallas Symphony season. Stan Ballinger, chairman of NIU's music department, called me to ask if I would be interested in interviewing for a position there. Stan had previously worked at Oberlin College with my uncle Louis Davidson. The job description he shared with my uncle fit my credentials perfectly, and Uncle Louis told him, "You are describing my nephew to a T." I was not then ready to give up my full-time profession of playing in a symphony orchestra, so I thanked Stan very much but declined the offer.

But that season things had begun to decline on the podium. The lack of decorum in the orchestra was frustrating for me. I found it hard to endure the incessant talking during rehearsals. So when Stan Ballinger called me back in 1968, I was happy to accept his invitation to come to DeKalb for an interview.

It was a dark, dreary night, raining like crazy, when I arrived in DeKalb, and having lived only in big cities it was quite a shock. I played a mini-recital for the faculty and then a series of interviews with the search committee. Within the week, I was offered the position of associate professor of trumpet and director of what would be the first jazz band ever at Northern Illinois University. But I had a dilemma: I had already signed a contract with Dallas for the 1968-69 season, and when I asked to be released from it, the conductor refused. I could have skipped out on my contract, and since I wasn't planning to play in another orchestra there would be no serious repercussions. But personal integrity is important to me, and I couldn't do that. I called the chair and asked if he could hold the position for one more year. He was able to accommodate me, and so I came to NIU in the fall of 1969, ready to assume my new life as a full-time educator.

The first week of school I had signs all over campus announcing that the newly-established NIU jazz ensemble would be holding auditions. I was surprised and pleased when sixty students showed up. Making the cut to twenty players was not easy, and this would prove to be a difficult process every year. I had promised we would play our first concert in six weeks, and in October 1969 jazz was born at NIU when we played at a student convocation.

The music department then had a controversial faculty member, Eleanor Tipton. Everyone either loved her or hated her; there was no middle ground. At our first concert, the program included a piece we called "E.T. Special." I explained to our students that this would be a special dedication to one of our faculty, and we launched into Count Basie's, "I Can't Stop Loving You." That evening Professor Tipton called me to say simply, "Mr. Modell, that was the nicest thing anyone has ever done for me." We became great friends, and she was a huge fan of the jazz ensemble, especially the youth concerts we did for over a thousand students every year in Sandburg Auditorium.

I introduced myself and the NIU jazz ensemble to the local community in some unusual ways. During my first year at NIU, I went into Sycamore to the local hardware store, owned by a wonderful family named Hepker. I walked up to the counter and told Mr. Hepker I wanted ten toilet plungers, five large ones and five small ones. Then I said, "You can keep the sticks." The look on his face was priceless. A few minutes later, I went back in and explained that I was starting a new jazz program at NIU, and plungers were required in a lot of Duke Ellington and Count Basie's music. They would be held at the end of the bell of the trumpets and trombones. By opening and closing them, you were able to get a "doo wah" effect.

Those first few years at NIU were devoted to recruiting high school students into our program in a town that was famous for barbed wire and corn-on-the-cob. Our funds were meager, so after I learned which high schools had the best jazz programs; I began to volunteer our jazz ensemble to visit and perform there, *if* the high school could pay for the bus and perhaps feed us lunch. At all-student assemblies, I would first acquaint the students with the music of Duke Ellington, Count Basie, Woody Herman, and Stan Kenton. We always made a point of finishing the concert with music that was popular with the high school students. Blood Sweat and Tears was a hot group at the time, and our wonderful vocalist, Jeff Jenkins, would emulate their vocal sound to the delight of the crowds. I also used the assembly to engage teachers and students in a contest to identify the well-known TV themes we would play. My larger purpose was always to whet the appetite of these young people for more big band music and concerts. Our programs were also very successful recruiting tools, and by my third year at Northern we had begun to attract some of the best students in Illinois.

That same year we had begun to compete in a jazz competition at a local college, where one of the most famous names in jazz, critiquing our group, handed back a comment sheet that contained his signature and nothing else. One of my colleagues later told me he had been in the hallway chatting with a friend during our entire performance. As we rode the bus back to DeKalb, the students were extremely disappointed, and they raised the question of how much it had cost us to attend this competition. They wondered if that money could be used in the future to bring in a guest artist to work with the ensemble and perhaps do a few tour concerts. This simple idea was the beginning of how the NIU jazz ensemble became the number one touring university jazz ensemble.

As an educator, I always tried to cultivate an atmosphere in which every student felt free to voice their ideas. I think one of the wisest things I did in the early years of working with the ensemble was to devote the last three days of the school year to an exchange of ideas on what we had accomplished that year, as well as what we could do to improve the program in the future. The first day I presented my own views, while the students gave their ideas on days two and three.

A wonderful example of how this exchange worked came when John Blane, one of the trombonists and one of the finest students I ever worked with, acknowledged that when we were performing we should have our best soloists front and center. However, during our rehearsals, every student should have the opportunity to learn the art of improvisation. The following year, we started every rehearsal with a 12-bar blues, where everyone had to stand up and blow a few choruses. This was just one of many ideas that came from our students to improve the program. The teacher became the student.

By the time our program was rolling, we regularly toured four imes a year: a four-day tour in early November, one over semester break of up to two weeks, a short tour in February, and then our one-week tour during spring break. I made sure that during my entire twenty-eight years at NIU, our students never missed more than three days of class each semester. These tours were enormously successful. They not only increased the number and caliber of students coming into NIU's music department, but our visits to schools all over Wisconsin, Iowa, Indiana and Illinois were always once-a-year happenings in these small towns.

Riding on the bus with us were some of the greatest jazz artists of our time. Dizzy Gillespie, Clark Terry, Louis Bellson, James Moody, and Marvin Stamm were just a few of the over fifty jazz greats I brought in to tour and teach our students. These musicians never failed to thrill us. My own personal favorite moment being the night my idol, Mel Torme, appeared with us at Joliet's beautiful Rialto Square Theater. Another magnificent night was Tito Puente's performance with our band at the Paramount Arts Center in Aurora.

Our tours acquired a predictable rhythm. Typically we'd leave in the morning, arrive at a high school, and haul in all of our instruments and sound equipment. We'd set up for the afternoon all-school assembly. After our performance, the high school jazz band would perform, and I would follow-up with a detailed critique of their playing. All the sections then split up to work out the critique with the members of the jazz ensemble. The high school music directors always told us these sectionals were the most valuable part of our visit. After that, our guest artist would give a clinic.

I deliberately made the dinner that followed into a memorable learning experience. We arranged for each high school musician to take their precise NIU counterpart home for dinner with them the drummer with the drummer, the bass player with the bass player. There the conversation blossomed and the kids asked our students endless questions For many of the students who came to study at NIU, we were the catalyst. Excitement built from the moment they sat and heard us in assembly and thought to themselves; I would really love to be a part of this ensemble.

In some ways, the most fulfilling and memorable of the jazz ensemble's many outreach efforts were our performances at Illinois correctional institutions. It all came about when in 1971, an NIU student came up to me after one of our concerts and told me he had just been released from Pontiac prison. "Boy," he remarked, "the guys at Pontiac would really love for you to come and play for them." I started to investigate this possibility, and we ended up playing a December concert there. I remember the trip down to Pontiac was hair-raising, with our bus driver Wilbur forced to drive on sheer ice for the entire trip.

We were happy to get there. It took an hour-and-a-half to move us from the first section of the prison, where we were taken into a room and frisked, to the area where our concert would take place. The guard who confiscated my package of gum told me he would let me take a revolver in before he would permit the gum, because prisoners could use it to mess up the prison's electric doors. While we waited, we could see the residents having visitors day, separated from their loved ones by a six-inch pane of glass, as they reached out to their children, their babies, their wives, and lovers. It made a sobering impression on us, seeing the inside of a maximum security prison for the first time.

Pontiac prison had seven cellblocks at the time, each with 110 men. Only one cell block was allowed to watch the concert, which would be recorded and then broadcast throughout the prison that evening. I had a long talk with the assistant warden who told me Pontiac would be a perfect place to recruit because so many prisoners came from Dunbar and Kenwood high schools in Chicago, schools with good jazz programs.

We started by playing three tunes without interruption, trying to get the feel of the place and calm down the nervousness in the room that was palpable. I then greeted them by saying, "Good afternoon, gentlemen. We are delighted to be at Pontiac to play for you today. I suppose you are all wondering why there are no black players in this band." (This was at the start of my NIU career.) Some guy in the back yelled out, "Because we're all here in the joint!" This broke up the place and broke the ice.

After the concert, I met an inmate named "Shoe," who had already served twelve years on a murder charge. I later found out his story: he was one of a group of five sixteen-year-olds who committed armed robbery, with a gun going off and Shoe taking the rap. He had been a tenor-sax player in high school, and he asked me if he could play with the band. The other connection was that Shoe was a friend of the NIU student who had first approached me about playing at Pontiac. I later arranged to have two Buddy Rich charts sent down for Shoe to learn, something that lent him stature at Pontiac. In the meantime, I let him rehearse with our band.

As I was sitting backstage, a Latino man joined me. He evidently worked there as a butcher, for his white apron was covered with blood. After a while when neither of us spoke, he looked at me and asked, "Are you playing any Latin music today?" "No," I replied, "but if I had known you wanted to hear that, I certainly would have prepared some." He introduced himself as Guadalupe, from New York City, and we got to know each other well.

In the early 1970's, I knew Guadalupe well enough to ask him when he was coming up for parole. He told me that it would be in 1997. To my "Why, what did you do?" he said, "I kill my wife; she talk too much," which as you can imagine set me back on my heels. We started corresponding, and I worked with the prison's priest, along with NIU music faculty member Al O'Connor, to send percussion instruments down to the prison: congas, timbales, claves, and bongos. I also sent reeds to Shoe so that his saxophone would be in good shape. He later asked if I would be willing to make a recording of my thoughts about his fitness to be assigned to a work-release program, which I was happy to do. "Shoe" was eventually put on work-release and finished his sentence. I later ran into him at a supermarket in DeKalb. He was living in small-town Esmond, Illinois, married with a wife and child

One of my most treasured letters was the very last one that Guadalupe wrote me from prison. In it he went through his whole life story starting with his childhood in el barrio at 110th Street and Fifth Avenue This was Spanish Harlem. It turned out Guadalupe knew a lot of the folks I had worked with when I was playing with Latin bands, includin all of the guys from our rehearsal space on 110th Street. .In his last paragraph, he wrote, "If I ever get out of the joint, I am going to find a beautiful woman who will cook me chicken and rice. We are going to make love, but if she talks too much, I kill her too." So much for rehabilitation!

The jazz ensemble also played at a medium security facility in Vienna, Illinois. One of the highlights of our concert there was a suite from the show "Jesus Christ Superstar." It included a section called "Ascension," described musically by Harmon muted trumpets and sliding trombones played very softly, giving the effect of an upward spiral. When the music stopped there were a few seconds of silence, after which the band broke into a Basie-like groove and had the audience yell out together "Yeah baby!" You cannot imagine what it sounded like for hundreds of people to do that at precisely the same moment. It was something I will never forget.

We also played regularly at the women's correctional facility in Dwight, Illinois. At one concert, the band delivered such a rousing version of Dizzy Gillespie's "Manteca" that the girls were dancing on the tables. The warden asked that we not play anything quite that exciting again!

Playing for prison audiences was a unique musical and personal experience. I feel these concerts were enormously important, not only for my students but for the true entertainment and fellowship that both the prisoners and the band members shared. A remark my son Christopher made about one of our appearances at the Dwight prison reveals what a great sense of humor he had. One of our concerts at Dwight happened to fall on my birthday. The women in the prison somehow got wind of this, and while I was announcing the next number they all stood up to sing "Happy Birthday" to me, a very sweet gesture. On our return concert the following year, as I related the story to my son Christopher, a young woman came up and asked me, "Ain't it your birthday?" "No," I replied, "but how nice of you to remember that it's around this time of year." When she questioned how old I was, I replied, "I'm 47," to which she responded, "You look good!" Christopher immediately quipped, "Dad, to anybody in prison, you'd look great!"

My son Joshua, an editor at the popular satiric newspaper "The Onion," was equally quick to respond to my account of a concert I performed in after I retired from NIU. My dear friend Keith Rudolph, masterful director of a great symphonic wind group at Penn High School in Mishawaka, Indiana, had lured me out of my Florida winter home to come north in January. To Josh's question "Dad, how did the concert go?" I responded, "You know, Josh, I have performed the aria "Nessun Dorma" from the opera "Turandot" probably thirty or forty times. It never failed that each time I played it, at least one woman has come backstage to tell me, "You made me cry!" Josh's take on this was, "Dad, the first time you play it right, that's not going to happen anymore!" I'm grateful that each of my sons has a great sense of humor.

My good friend Lew Soloff was one of the most popular trumpeters in America during the early 1970s, playing with the enormously popular "Blood, Sweat, and Tears." Despite his busy schedule, I was able to bring him to NIU for a trumpet clinic. While Lew was visiting, I delivered one of my funniest lines without trying to be funny. It was sheer naiveté.

Lew had asked me to arrange for him to meet with the legendary Adolph "Bud" Herseth, iconic first trumpeter of the Chicago Symphony Orchestra. I called Bud, and along with CSO second trumpet Vince Cichowicz, we all met for food and drink at Miller's Pub after the symphony's Thursday night concert. Lew and I drove back that night to my home in Sycamore, and after awhile, Lew looked at me and said, "Hey Ronnie, I've got some great Columbian Gold!" "Lew," I told him, "I never drink coffee before I go to sleep." I obviously had no idea what he was talking about. To me, Columbian Gold sounded like a cup of coffee!

That evening at Miller's Pub was really special. After Bud Herseth had consumed two or three Heinekens, all of a sudden his glasses slid down on his nose and he would begin to regale us with marvelou Fritz Reiner stories. At one point, I asked Bud, "You know, a lot of my students and I wonder about how you play four concerts of the same program—Thursday night, followed by Friday afternoon, Saturday nigh and then Milwaukee on Monday night. Let's say 'Petroushka' is on th program, and on Thursday night you have probably played it as well as it can be played. Now you have to repeat it three more times—how do you get yourself up to do it again?" Without hesitating, Herseth replied, "I have never left the stage of any performance feeling as if I have done all to the music that I wanted to." What a surprise to hear this from the greatest symphonic trumpeter of our time! Herseth turned to Vince and said, "How about you, Vince?" Vince shook his head no. Lew responded in kind. "How about you, Ron?" Without hesitation, I said, "Three times!" And boy, those guys went under the table. As we stood out on the pavement at one in the morning, it was ironic that it was Bud and Vince asking *Lew* for autographed photos of him with "Blood, Sweat, and Tears" for their children.

One evening during the 1970-71 school year, I heard for the first time a magnificent choir rehearsing in the old music building. I was immediately struck by the enthusiasm and excitement in their music. Opening the door to find out who was making this glorious sound, I discovered the NIU Black Choir. As I sat and listened to them rehearse, I began to think how exciting it would be to feature the choir with the jazz ensemble. At the end of the rehearsal, I introduced myself to the choir director Ken and asked if we could meet to talk about putting our two groups together. Once Ken agreed, I immediately called my dear friend Harry Max in New York City, and commissioned him to do three arrangements featuring the Black Choir with the ensemble.

The first joint rehearsal turned out to be a rather nervous one. I felt some hostility from some of the choir members. In the days before the rehearsal, I had gotten my students very excited about our joint project, and now I was shocked by the tension in the room. This was going to be a real test of having music serve as the catalyst in bringing our two groups together.

I truly believe that the selections Ken and I made, along with the great writing of Harry Max, accomplished what I had originally thought was a great idea. We began the choir set with "Go Down Moses," followed by "We've Only Just Begun," and concluding with "What the World Needs Now." The result was a standing ovation by the 498 people who jammed the O'Connell Theater that evening. We received the same response the next night from another capacity audience. After each performance, it was tremendously rewarding to see the members of the ensemble and the choir embracing each other, glowing with pride in their collaboration and what they had brought to their audiences. This was a great learning experience for all of us, and it remains one of my fondest memories of NIU.

In 1974, we made jazz history at NIU when Duke Ellington played his last concert at what was then the Holmes Student Center Ballroom. I first met Duke in the late 1960's when he conducted the Dallas Symphony Orchestra, playing his piece "The Golden Apple." Like all of his music, a sheer joy to perform. I have some wonderful home movies taken of that evening in his dressing room.

He was quite ill by the time he played at NIU, and shortly before the concert began his son Mercer came to find me and took me to his room. It was a shock to see the shape he was in. He was sitting slumped over on the bed, but as I came in he got up and gave me a big hug. We reminisced a bit about Dallas, and I got a chuckle out of him when I said he was the only conductor in my entire symphonic career that started the orchestra with the vocal prompt "123123." We had a special T-shirt made for him, the front of which quoted one of his most famous lines, delivered to each audience he performed for: "We love you madly." The photograph of him shows how he had turned the shirt around, so the words on the back, "The NIU Jazz Ensemble," were visible. Soon after his death, the room in which he performed was renamed the Duke Ellington Ballroom, a fitting commemoration of a great American jazz icon and his connection to NIU's own jazz history.

Each summer from 1974 to 1978, I hosted the national stage band camps on our NIU campus, directed by Ken Morris. Our first week was always devoted to big band ensembles, and it featured an all-star faculty. Some of the biggest names in jazz would spend a week with perhaps a hundred students, sharing with them the valuable experiences of their musical lives. Can you imagine a young high school student mixing it up with Louis Bellson, Phil Wilson, Lou Marini, Wes Hensel, Roger Pemberton or Ashley Alexander?

While the first week was relatively easy to run—I merely had to find two or three large ensemble rooms where the big bands could rehearse—the second week was formidable. Week two was run by Jamey Aebersold, one of the most influential jazz educators in the country. The 200-plus students were all part of combos. I had the daunting task of coming up with twenty-four rooms, each of which had to contain a piano, a drum set, a guitar amp, and a bass amp. The faculty for week two was also made up of great jazz artists and teachers, some of whom had requests that were not always easy to fulfill. The great pianist Ronnie Matthews, for example, insisted on having a studio with two grand pianos facing each other.

Working with Jamey was always a joy, and whenever any of the thirty-or-so faculty got a bit out of line, he was wonderful in the way he settled them down. I do remember vividly, however, a time when a faculty member approached me to say they were all getting tired of working so hard without a break. They badly needed some fun and diversion, and they asked me if I could get ahold of some stag movies we could watch? That night we gathered in the room of a great jazz bassist at the Holmes Student Center. Try to picture two-dozen people in one small hotel room and the air thick with smoke. I started the film, and as the guys watched and made remarks that only musicians would make, there suddenly was a knock at the door.

I immediately flipped off the projector, someone opened the door, and after the funk cleared, there stood the very classy and laid-back Jamey Aebersold. "Hi fellas, what's going on?" Our great bassist, decked out in a beautiful sweater vest and smoking his pipe, told Jamey, "Ron was showing us some movies of his trip to Yellowstone." There was a pause before Jamey replied, "That's nice; I'll see you in the morning." After the initial roar, I flipped the projector back on.

You will understand my great admiration and respect for Jamey when I tell you this story about a party he and his wife hosted at their home. All of the guests were white, except for one young lady, Kathy, who had come as a date with one of the guests. You could sense the discomfort in the room—remember, this was the 1970s—but Jamey knew just what to do. When Kathy's date went to get them drinks, he sat down on the couch next to her and said loudly, "Hi Kathy. I'm Jamey, and Pat tells me you're black." Of course the room roared and everyone relaxed—another wonderful evening at the Aebersold's.

Our first European tour in 1984-85 was a landmark event for the band. It was a nineteen-day tour on which I took along my fifteen-year-old son Christopher. We arrived in Amsterdam after an all-night flight. I remember being so exhausted that I looked out of our window and commented to the band, "Have you ever seen so many goddamned foreign cars?" Tired though we were, I took the students to the Reichsmuseum to see the magnificent Rembrandts.

That night as we walked Amsterdam's cobblestone streets, gawking like the tourists we were, we came upon a shop lit up with neon lights and all kinds of things in the window. The sign read "Sex Shop," and my son Christopher asked me under his breath, "Dad, do you think I could have a year's advance on my allowance?' To which I responded, "Chris, you are not taking anything home with you and you are not leaving anything here!"

Although the band worked hard, we always kept a feeling of looseness and fun. The last thing that every band in my twenty-eight years at NIU would hear from me before they performed was, "Go out there and have a good time! Enjoy yourselves!"

They certainly did that when, back in the 1980's, NIU's Student Association ran their annual Erotic Film Festival in Sandburg Auditorium, a whole week of X-rated entertainment. It was also a smart business move, for in that week they pulled in enough money to show first-run movies on weekends there, with free student admission, during the rest of the school year. The night the Festival screened "Deep Throat" the band was getting ready to go on stage in the Duke Ellington Ballroom where two thousand people filled every seat and others stood in the back to watch. Just as the Jazz Ensemble was about to walk on stage, I told them my spontaneous idea to have some fun. The band never knew what to expect from me! After our first number, I said to the audience, "Ladies and gentlemen, when you get on an airplane, before it takes off the review the flight number and destination. Tonight I want to announce that if anyone came here thinking they were going to see Linda Lovelace in 'Deep Throat,' you should move to Sandburg Auditorium behind us." The audience snickered and laughed while I kept checking my watch for a minute or so. When I turned around, the entire band had left, which got a hilarious response from our audience. No wonder we earned this tribute from the great flugelhorn player Marvin Stamm, the soloist on Paul McCartney's "Uncle Albert: "There is a true affection and total support in this group for everyone. I've never seen a group so much for one another."

I had the pleasure of teaching a wonderful pianist, Karl Montzka, who got me twice, to the great delight of the ensemble. Karl came from a very musical family; his father had conducted the Kishwaukee Symphony Orchestra. I was telling the band about a funny story connected with trombonist Phil Wilson, one of the early soloists at NIU. Some six weeks after his concert here, I picked up the phone at 6:50 a.m. to hear an older woman's voice in a strong country accent, "Mr. Modell? You know, that fella you had playin' the trombone? I saw that concert and I didn't like all them extree notes he put in 'Poor Butterfly.'" Phil Wilson had done an incredible improvisation of that classic tune. I responded, "Well, I will tell him if he ever comes back not to do that." Following up on this strange call, because I was really fascinated that someone would call me and talk like that, I discovered that she was the Sycamore town drunk, at which point Karl immediately yelled, "But my mother's doing much better now!" Great line, and it broke up the band.

Karl did it again, during a lull in our rehearsal when I was looking over something in the score. "Hey Mode!" he called from the piano. ("The Mode" was my nickname for many years, bestowed on me by Dave Katz.) "Did you ever hear the four different types of reactions that women have when they are being made love to?" "No," I said, "What are they?" "Well, there is the positive," Karl began, and proceeded to go, "Yes, yes, yes!" very passionately. "There is the negative, "No, no, no!" Then, you have the religious, "Oh God, oh God!" He finished with, "And then there are the women who fake orgasms—"Yes Mode, yes Mode, I love it Mode!" This was the kind of relaxed rapport I always wanted students to experience during our relationship.

Karl and many other students, certainly got in their zingers, and I reciprocated. In August 1988, a young, talented trumpet student walked into my office, some weeks before the semester had even begun. A graduate of Ron Carter's jazz program at Lincoln High School in East St. Louis, Tony Wiggins was not yet eighteen years old. He wanted to enroll in NIU and play with the jazz ensemble. His grades and ACT score did not meet the requirements. But after listening to him play, I arranged to have him admitted on a one-year trial. I had already worked out a plan with the admissions office that if I found a very talented student whose scores were not up to par, they could be admitted on probation for one year. As long as they maintained a C average, they would be permitted to continue.

During Tony's sophomore year, I announced to the band that the following morning I would be having cataract surgery and would not be back until the following Monday. To my surprise, at 9 a.m. on Monday morning, there was a knock on my studio door. I opened it, and there stood Tony. "Hey Mode, how did your cataract surgery go?" I slowly removed my eye-patch and gasped, "Oh my God, Tony, you're black!" He had one of the most infectious laughs I've ever heard, and the sound of it opened all the studio doors on the first floor.

One evening the jazz ensemble performed with guest artist Vincent DiMartino, a magnificent trumpeter. My dear father was sitting in the audience in NIU's President's box. I made a point of telling the crowd that my dad was there, and had come all the way from New Jersey and that Vinnie wanted to dedicate the next number to him, a great tune called "Concerto for Cootie." As I stood in front of the band and lifted my arms to give the downbeat, I heard Vinnie DiMartino say under his breath, "I didn't know your dad's first name was Cootie!" I just fell apart. My dad's name, of course, was Nathan. Vinnie's timing and his beautiful delivery of that line was one of the few times that I ever really lost it on stage and had to take some time to pull myself back together!

One of the things I worked at in building NIU's jazz program was to make sure our students had the opportunity to write and perform their own original compositions or to arrange music that they truly.

loved I was always touched and amazed by the reaction of our audiences to these student pieces, especially at our NIU concerts. After the jazz ensemble recorded its first album in 1973—what would be the first of thirteen such albums—the publisher of the jazz magazine "Downbeat," Chuck Suber, asked me "Why didn't you do some Basie or Ellington; why so many student compositions?" My response was that we weren't about to play Basie and Ellington better than Basie and Ellington. These recordings were also extremely valuable for students to submit in their future interviews. I also made a point of seeing that whenever a student's work was recorded or performed, they would be at the podium. What pride I felt when recently learning that one of our best students and composers from the late 1980s, Ed Partyka, had nine of his students finish in the top twelve, in a world contest for jazz composition. Ed's contributions to jazz in Germany and Austria have done much to spread NIU's global reputation for jazz.

That reputation continued to crest. A real breakthrough came in 1978 at the National Association of Jazz Educators in Dallas, where the NIU jazz ensemble was the featured group on Saturday night. Dizzy Gillespie was our soloist. Afterwards, people flooded the stage, everyone asking us, "Where the hell is DeKalb, Illinois?"

The corporate world was also paying attention as our graduates began to land jobs in the entertainment industry. Walt Disney World executive Bob Radock paid tribute, writing, "For years, we have hosted your sensational bands, hired many of your students to work for us, and sought your counsel on many occasions because of your expertise in jazz education." Executives recognized the extraordinary teamwork they saw embodied in the jazz ensemble. After performing for Motorola, vice president Michael Winston praised us in a letter: "Led by Ron Modell and Antonio Garcia, the NIU Jazz Ensemble demonstrated the principles of creativity, leadership, individual skills, and the harmony and synergy achieved through teamwork."

In 1979, I was interviewed on the "Studs Terkel" show along with jazz drummer Louis Bellson, and the next morning I received a phone call from WTTW producer Michael Hirsh. He had enjoyed the interview and now wanted to produce a documentary for public television on what he later called, "A Year in the Life of the Greatest College Jazz Band in America." I disputed the title, but Michael insisted. When the show premiered, with Dizzy Gillespie on the voice-over, I made sure Dizzy referred to us as, "*one* of the best college bands in America."

The documentary aired in 1983 and was broadcast nationwide; I received fan mail from as far away as Alaska and Hawaii. The show really put us on the map, bringing to the ensemble and Northern Illinois University national recognition. It also captured two Chicago Emmys for best performance on camera that year, commemorating the film's explosive and exuberant drum duel between Louis Bellson and our own drummer Vern Spevak. NIU's presidents consistently reiterated that, as one of them put it, "the NIU jazz ensemble is the greatest public relations we have." There were new faces every year, but all the students came with the knowledge that they were there to uphold an increasingly great tradition. There was never a year that they failed to do that.

Like anyone else, I struggled with some students, and often when I did so I tried to make the entire ensemble part of the solution. Some time during the 1980's, a freshman student from one of the suburbs entered NIU as a music major, but more specifically to become a member of the NIU jazz ensemble. This young man was as brash, arrogant, and abrasive as anyone I had ever met. During audition week, he went right up to one of the players from last year's ensemble and told him, "I'm going to have your chair this year."

He did not make the ensemble that year but did win a chair the next year. As we approached the final week of the fall semester, the other four players in his section came to me in my office and said, "If he goes on the winter tour, we're not going." I told the four of them, you know that we are committed to clinics and concerts for those ten days plus we have engaged the services of a well-known jazz soloist.

I told them I realized that this young man had been very difficul to work with but that I wanted all of them to seriously consider why he acted that way. You have to ask yourself, "Why does he act this way none of you do." "Here's what I would like you to do," I said. "On th tour I would like for each and every one of you, on separate nights, to invite him out for a cup of coffee, a coke, or whatever you like to drink. I want you all to try to help this colleague of yours to be a better person."

At our spring concert, we traditionally gave out an award to the one person in the ensemble who had contributed the most to the successes we enjoyed. What an incredible feeling I had the following year, when this young man won he award in his junior year. He has gone on to a great career as a music educator, and I could not be more proud of any graduate that has gone through the jazz ensemble program.

Once again during the 1980's, I encountered a situation that I had not experienced before. Two new students had come into the ensemble with completely negative attitudes. My first instinct was to respond as a father and a teacher. My thought was, I will get them off the road they are traveling down and set them on the right path to a successful and happy life. The more I tried, the worse it got. While I had always felt like I couldn't wait to rehearse with the jazz ensemble, now I dreaded going to that class. The year-and-a-half that I suffered through this experience, one in which I felt like a failure, taught me a very important lesson. You cannot help *everyone* you meet in life; not everyone is *savable*. What I should have done, and thank goodness the situation never came up again, was to have early on called these students into my office, explained to them how the program was run, and then tell them, "If I don't see an immediate improvement in your attitude, let's shake hands, and you go find yourself another band to play with." One of the students saw the light and has gone on to a great career as one of the premier musicians in the Chicago-land area. My feeling of failure was erased when, a few years after his graduation, the student called me on the phone and apologized profusely for his behavior. I never heard one word from the other student, and I understand his life may not have gone the way he would have liked it to go.

Our successes were inseparable from our philosophy of always going out there and having fun. The only way to be able to do that, however, was by being well-prepared. Preparation builds confidence. It's what I would call the 50/50 approach to making music. The first fifty percent is to meet the challenge of technically mastering the music, to the point of where someone could wake you at three in the morning, put the instrument in your hand, and you could play it. The challenge of the other fifty percent is to take those black, dead, inanimate forms on white paper and make the musical notes come to life.

I always tried to impress upon students that they should enjoy every moment of their high school and college years, truly some of the best times of their lives. This is when you have lots of people looking after you; I would say, trying to help you to be successful. It's almost like being in the womb because so many people are trying to nurture your talent and set you in the right direction. I think the music field is truly special that way; in fact, in any of the arts there always seems to be a special fraternity or sorority of people that really care for each other. It was always important for me to make sure students knew that most of their teachers deeply cared about sharing what they knew. I urged students to pick their teachers' brains and get as much out of them as possible. I would tell them, over and over, "Enjoy this time!" After you graduate and get out into that big, bad world, you're not in the warm safe womb any more. Here at NIU, you are going to be playing with some of the best musicians you have ever played with, sharing moments like you will never experience again.

The title for this memoir came to me as soon as I decided to write it.

Early in my career at NIU, jazz trombonist Phil Wilson, one of our first soloist-clinicians, heard me fooling around in rehearsal, singing that great Peggy Lee tune "I Love Being Here with You." Phil made me a ten-dollar bet that I would not have the nerve to sing it on stage that evening. Despite never having sung it publicly, I couldn't resist the challenge and I accepted his wager.

When I sang it, I changed one word: the "I" became "We," a wonderful way to tell the audience how much we enjoyed being there with them. With a beautiful arrangement by Phil Kelly, in one minute and forty seconds, we could say from the heart what we felt as a band. The song became the NIU Jazz Ensemble's signature, and we ended every concert with it.

Each year's new ensemble took it as a challenge to create a unique interpretation of our classic closer. Like the old big bands, physical showmanship was the order of the day—the trombones would sway back and forth, their horns pointed to the sky while the trumpets sliced up and down in a vertical motion. Because I was singing and facing our audience, I missed the incredible show going on right behind me. It wasn't until years later, watching videos of our concerts, that I could finally see how much of themselves our students were putting into it. No doubt about it: the song defined the NIU Jazz Ensemble. We always "loved bein' there with you."

Ron,

The originality, creativity, musicianship and performance of this NIU album are of the highest quality. But you, as the leader, have made the most important contribution! It is your guidance, inspiration, and leadership that have made all this possible. I salute you!

Stan Kenton
Liner Notes for NIU Jazz Ensemble's
"Fly by Night"

PEDAGOGY, OR SHARING ALL YOU KNOW

In 1997, Jim Rohner, publisher of "The Instrumentalist" magazine, approached me to write a monthly column. I was honored because I have always considered "The Instrumentalist" to be an important magazine that serves a great purpose in music education. Years later, when I told Jim that I was about to embark on writing my memoirs, he implored me to be sure to include a chapter on pedagogy. He pointed out future music educators need to know how you were able to develop both a highly successful jazz program at NIU, and mentor your trumpet students to professional careers, both as performers and educators, always meeting the highest professional standards.

My pedagogical career began when I was in the Tulsa Philharmonic. I started teaching young students, usually beginning around the age of ten. I told the parents of my young students that fifteen minutes a day of a disciplined practice routine, would be enough to help them begin to develop not only their embouchure (or lip positions), but their musical abilities as well.

One of the most important things in teaching younger students is to have some kind of musical reward at the end of each lesson. At that time, Herb Alpert and the Tijuana Brass were tremendously popular, maybe the hottest group in the nation. I was able to find the Tijuana Brass books, which came in a set, and this music really excited my young students and bolstered their enthusiasm for doing the first part of the lesson. There we would go through the basics, practicing some long tones and learning their scales. Like most teachers, I would write out certain exercises. But, you can be sure every student I taught was going to be a disciple of the Schlossberg "Daily Drills and Studies" method, which is the same system under which I was first taught.

At first I shared the common misconception, based on the Arban method, that the mouthpiece should be placed on two-thirds of the lower lip and one-third of the upper lip. Over time, however, I became certain through talking with other teachers and players all over the world, that when you start with a student, you need to allow them to find a place that fits them best. Of course, if that place is completely out of whack you make the adjustments. In most cases, 50-50 is a good place to start, and then the natural thing will happen.

Before any brass player begins their practice, it is important to buzz the mouthpiece for thirty seconds or so before beginning to play, in order to get the air and the vibrations moving. I was never taught by any of my great teachers to do mouthpiece practice, perhaps because the great Schlossberg did not teach this method. It wasn't until I was well into my forties or early fifties, when I took some lessons with Arnold Jacobs, the fabulous tubist with the Chicago Symphony, that I began thinking about using the mouthpiece as he did. On his way to work, he would have the mouthpiece in his right hand while driving with his left, playing everything from the Star Spangled Banner to the repertoire scheduled for that day's rehearsal.

I am now convinced that mouthpiece practice is essential to becoming an accomplished player. I never did get to study with the highly respected west-coast teacher Jimmy Stamp, but I understand that it was an essential part of his teaching. I believe that the current trumpet teacher at the Eastman School of Music, Jim Thompson, whom I admire tremendously, is also an ardent advocate of mouthpiece practice. In my daily routine as a young player, my teachers instructed me to buzz the mouthpiece for about thirty seconds: start playing a tone, tongue a few notes, and then use it as a fire engine, making a kind of "Whooooooo!" siren sound up and down, up and down.

After buzzing the mouthpiece, I would start at the beginning of Schlossberg, with the long tones of low-C, which we now know today is not the best way to start. Beginning in low-C relaxed the embouchure—the position in which you set your mouth and face—more than was necessary. The second-line G for the B-flat trumpet, I discovered, was the better place to start. My top priority was to immediately strive for a good tone.

Not one of my teachers ever explained proper breathing to me. It was only after I finished my fourth season with the Tulsa Philharmonic that I went to New York to study with Frank Venezia and learned something about how to breathe. I think my life as a trumpet player would have been significantly different if any of the other great trumpet teachers I had would have taught me how to breathe correctly. In retrospect, I think because I immediately had a beautiful sound and played well right away, my teachers assumed I was breathing properly.

I had no idea of the importance of using my abdominal muscles. In our very first lesson, Frank Venezia really opened my eyes to the fact that all these years I had been playing by using too much mouthpiece pressure, rather than using the air column properly. When I came back for my second lesson and played the exercises that Frank had written out for me, I complained to him that I was experiencing a lot of pain in my abdomen, my back, and my side. He was very happy and told me, "Good! Good! Now you are using muscles you have never used before."

Regardless of their teaching techniques, every great brass player agrees on these key points. You still have to put the instrument up to your mouth. You still have to buzz your lips. You still have to push air through the horn. The approaches may be different, but these are always the basics of playing a brass instrument.

I remember the late great Bud Herseth, trumpeter with the Chicago Symphony, saying that he did not like to use the word "register." Herseth felt that all the notes were the same. Many brass players used to go to Orchestra Hall with a pair of binoculars to watch Herseth. There was almost no movement when he was playing; red face, yes, but no movement in the embouchure. One of the most defining statements anybody could make about the perfect embouchure, while not thinking about the concept of register, would be what Maynard Ferguson did in his album "A Message from Newport." On one track, he played one of the greatest big-band charts ever, "Framework for the Blues." On this track, Maynard's very last entrance, he hits a double high-C and, without removing the trumpet or mouthpiece from his lips, uses a little improvisation to go from double high-C all the way down to low F-sharp the lowest possible note on the trumpet

What else can I say? In a brass player's perfect world, the hardest notes still feel like you're playing the easiest ones. For giants like

Bud Herseth and Maynard Ferguson, every single note they played on the trumpet had the same relaxed feeling as I did when playing an easy note like middle-G. .

A defining experience for my own playing was studying with the great teacher Don Jacoby, to perfect his concept of the "pivot note." At the time, I was playing principal trumpet in Dallas, and we were rehearsing "Pagliacci" in the Dallas Civic Opera In this opera, the very first entrance for the B-flat trumpet starts on the B-flat above the staff. You have to work your way down, never taking the horn away from your lips or resetting your embouchure. I was having a tough time with it, and Don Jacoby said to me, "Well, when you get ready to play that first B-flat above the staff, are you setting your embouchure for that B-flat above the staff?" "Of course," I replied. Don said, "This is where we change your life. Now we are going to introduce you to the pivot note."

The pivot note concept was to simply look at a passage, find its highest and its lowest notes, and then set your embouchure for the middle. In this case, that would have been a third-line B-flat. Don Jacoby then had me play three, four, or five middle-B-flats in a row and, without taking the horn off my mouth or the mouthpiece from my lips, he would have me start at the high B-flat and play the passage all the way down. It worked like magic because now everything felt like I was in my perfect range, right in the middle of the horn.

Don Jacoby also cured me of my chronic apprehension about playing the famous solo near the end of "Der Rosenkavalier," a popular part of the Dallas Symphony's repertoire. I dreaded it, because it was one of the few pieces in my entire career in which I lacked the confidence in my ability to play it without cracking it. It didn't help that I was playing such challenging music on a B-flat trumpet, instead of an easier C or D trumpet. After Don had me apply the pivot note theory of finding the middle ground, I never missed it again. I even began to anticipate and love playing this solo.

Still another critical aspect of trumpet technique is how a musician initially "attacks" the first note in any passage. As a teacher, I quickly learned to never make a general statement and claim, "This is the only way you can do something," because as soon as you say this, someone will come along and do it ass-backwards, or completely differently, and get it done just fine. The one thing I have felt very strongly about is that when you make the first attack of any passage, you must use the consonant "T." For instance, on a low note, think of "tah"; in the middle range, think "tu", and for the upper, think "ti." I know there are many teachers who believe in simply blowing air and vibrating the lips to begin the tone. In his book, *Trumpet Techniques,* my uncle Louis Davidson advocated instead a three-part process of attack. Step one, you put the horn up to your lips in complete repose, without setting any embouchure. Steps two and three happen simultaneously. If it is going to be a middle-G, then you simply get your tongue right behind your top teeth, and as soon as you take your breath, your tongue immediately strikes behind the top teeth with the syllable "tu."

In my experience, one of the greatest challenges is to effectively attack a high note softly. My own approach was to use the same forceful stroke of the tongue as you would for a loud note, while simultaneously controlling the amount of air that is released. This gave me the psychological confidence that made it unnecessary to try to sneak into any soft attack, an approach that too many players rely on.

My whole philosophy in teaching the trumpet technique of "tonguing" was that if you could master the legato single-tongue— where you have no break in the sound, but simply sustain a note and interrupt it with the correct syllable—then the art of articulation would never be a problem. In order to play the legato single tongue, the student must practice long tones, interrupting each one after the initial T attack with the *du* syllable. For example, start on an easy middle-G and proceed to sound out "tu, du, du, du, du" without any interruption to the air column. As the student progresses, the *du* syllable becomes shorter and in time changes into a simple tongue staccato which still retains the sound of the original long tone. The same principle holds true for the more advanced techniques of multiple tonguing, or double and triple-tonguing.

During the twenty-eight years that I taught at Northern Illinois University, we had three or four days a year when students would come to audition for entrance into the School of Music. It was amazing that when I would ask any student on a brass instrument to play a major scale, if their articulation was such that they had never been taught about legato single-tonguing, many times it came out sounding like a motorboat, a sort of "putt-putt-putt." You would hear the scale with very short abbreviated notes, with no quality of sound to them or really good pitch. On the other hand, students who had been taught about legato-style tonguing would play a scale that sounded very different.

When I was studying with my teachers and being assigned the long-tone Schlossberg exercises, I didn't realize it at the time, but every few months they would have me shorten the stroke, so I would still retain the beautiful sound of a legato tone just being interrupted. They were teaching me all of the different articulations, so if I needed to play something heavily punctuated with a *marcato,* they would have me do that. It was a learning process that I didn't even realize was going on, but the foundation was the fact that I could legato single-tongue, and I carried this forward into all the playing that I ever did. I was always very comfortable in being able to play a long legato and then cut it short to a very staccato sound, while still having it come out with a good tone quality, a good definition of pitch. Never, except in rare occasions, such as a Stravinsky piece, would the tone become *secco*, or a very dry short sound. I used that kind of sound in Stravinsky's "Firebird," and I also remember using it in "The Sorcerer's Apprentice.

I also used *portamento* tonguing, which is a slur line on top of notes with dots underneath them. To me, this tonguing produced the most beautiful articulation. I always thought of Felix Mendelssohn's "Fingal's Cave Overture," or the second movement in Beethoven's first symphony.

It became absolutely imperative with my students that they master the legato single-tongue because that was the key, the common denominator to all tonguing articulations. When we got into multiple tonguing double and triple-tonguing using the famous studies in the Arban book for some reason, all the teachers and players I ever talked to taught triple-tongue before they taught double-tongue. You started with a "tu, tu, ku," accenting the "ku" very heavily. In the first two notes, there was no interruption of the air column, simply a long tone.

During my tour with Cornelia Otis Skinner's "Paris 90," our conductor Nat Shilkret introduced me to one of the greatest trumpeters of our time, Rafael Mendez. He invited me to his home the next morning for a private lesson and asked me what I wanted him to help me with. I said simply, "You are known as the world's greatest double and triple-tongue player. Could you show me your secret?" What an astounding shock when he immediately went over to his books, pulled out the Arban volume, and turned to page 155, saying, "You start by going 'tu tu ku, tu tu ku" with a heavy accent on the 'ku.' You are just introducing a new syllable into your mouth and into your playing, and you must heavily accent it without breaking the rhythm." It usually took my students about eight weeks before they could triple-tongue at a fast tempo. The easiest part of triple-tonguing, of course, was that the same note was repeated over and over. The difficulty comes when the notes start to change. And it gets tricky when the fingers have to coordinate with the tongue. Mendez pointed out to me that most Spanish-speaking people, and Polish people as well, always had phenomenal double and triple-tonguing, simply because of their native languages. In Spanish, many words begin with a "K" articulation, but this is far more rare in English. Once again, perfecting the legato single-tongue can do nothing but lead you to the greatest results in all the articulations on a brass instrument you will be called upon to do for the rest of your musical life.

I had my pre-war French Besson trumpet in a little cloth gig bag which I took out and prepared to play. Rafael took out his Olds trumpet—he was a big sponsor for the Olds company—and proceeded to do his warm-up with *pedal tones*, something I had never done in my life going up three octaves with tremendous flexibility. After five minute of this, I started to put my horn back in its bag. Rafael looked shocke and asked me what I was doing. "Do you really expect me to pla something after what I just heard?" I asked him. He said he had hope it would inspire me, so I got out my horn again, and we started workin on triple-tonguing.

Something else that really interested me during our lesson was that I noticed that so many of your solos were written in keys with four or five sharps. Why was that? He told me that when he started his study in Mexico, unlike American students who begin in the simple key of C major (which has no sharps or flats), he was immediately immersed in music with key signatures of many sharps or flats. This kind of training also contributed to his unusually strong third valve finger. American beginners spend so much time in the key of C that their first two valve fingers are usually much stronger than their weaker third valve finger. Rafael's third finger was just as strong as his first two. Another bonus was that, for recording purposes, keys with many sharps give the trumpet a much more brilliant sound.

As I came to my lessons each morning with Rafael Mendez in his Culver City house next to the MGM studios, I noticed a big jar in the entryway. He went over to the jar and took out something that at the time I didn't know was a jalapeno pepper. He took a bite and invited me to try it. Not knowing any better, I took a taste and thought my tongue was coming right out of my mouth! "Wow!" I exclaimed. "That was hot!" Rafael Mendez replied, "Yes, it gets you up in the morning, gets you right up, gets you feeling good."

One of the things that I prided myself on during my career was that I had achieved a true *pianissimo* on the trumpet. In a big auditorium, I could play *pianissimo* and the note would be heard by the person in the last row. It took a lot of practicing at the dynamic, just as you would practice a good *fortissimo*. Sir Georg Solti himself gave me some wonderful constructive criticism at the conclusion of his season with us in Dallas, as conductor, telling me, "The one thing I would like to see you do, is when you play *fortissimo* to have you produce the same beauty of sound that you do when you play *pianissimo*. He asked me if I had ever played in a church, and of course I had played in many. Maestro Solti said to think of the quality of sound you get in a beautiful church with exceptional acoustics. The one thing that should be in your mind at all times when playing *fortissimo* is that you are never playing loud for loud's sake, but rather that you are imagining the beautiful sound of *fortissimo* as if it were being played softly. The beauty of sound has to be in your mind and come through the horn, just as you would with a *pianissimo*

.   It really did work. At many clinics, I would play the opening of the Tchaikovsky fourth symphony loud for loud's sake, and then I would play it loud the way it should have been played. I think students were amazed by the striking difference, a strident ugly sound as opposed to a round beautiful sound, yet both with the same *fortissimo* dynamic.

My main objective in teaching was always something my uncle Louis taught me: that whether you were playing one note, a scale, or a concerto, it had to be musical. Whenever my students played a scale, whether in the practice room or for a final jury, it was not simply running up and down the scale to show off technical prowess, it was a musical event. When given a choice, I would have my students slur a two-octave scale, making a crescendo when ascending and a decrescendo when descending, always insisting it be musical.

In the hundreds of clinics that I have conducted in my lifetime, the main lesson I have always tried to put forth is that there are two halves to musical performance. The first half is learning the music well enough to play it flawlessly from a technical standpoint. This is the easy part, for now we even have computers and synthesizers that can be made to do that. The second part is much harder: to make the music come to life and project to the audience or to yourself something beautiful. I have emphasized to my students that when you go out to perform, always know that the audience comes in devoid of feelings, and it is your responsibility to give them something to take home with them that they didn't possess when they first arrived. It is never enough to merely play all the right notes—you can do this yet still not achieve the rewards of making music. To make music, you have to make those notes come alive, to project feelings and emotion. The ultimate goal is to project your own joy and exuberance in making music. This entire process is applicable to any discipline.

Dr. Robert Long, a Dallas psychiatrist whose son I instructed in trumpet, put all of this in perspective during a conversation we had about the career of Adolph Herseth. Dr. Long did not know anything about music, but he went to all the concerts he could, whether symphonic, opera, or jazz. He just loved music. I commented that if Herseth missed a note, the orchestra would probably turn around to see if he was still alive. What Dr. Long said that night helped me for the rest of my career. "I don't know about Mr. Herseth," he said, "but you know if ten percent of the time you leave a performance feeling as though no one could have ever played as well as you just did, and another ten percent of the time you leave wanting to throw your trumpet against the wall, well, neither of those ten percents counts for very much." He went on to say that although you always aim for one-hundred percent perfection, if you can manage to get into the ninetieth percentile in your playing, you've achieved as much success as any human being can expect. All kinds of things can impact your performance, from ill health and personal issues, to world crisis, severe weather, etc.

Rich Matteson, one of the premier jazz educators, told a gathering of band directors, "If a major league baseball player gets three hits out of ten times at bat, he is seen as a success. If a quarte back completes six out of ten passes, he is also a success. Now think about your ensembles, a hundred-piece band, a sixty-piece band or a hundred-piece orchestra. Think of the incredible percentage of accuracy that your students give you every day, at every concert, or better yet, imagine each student only getting three to six notes correct out of every ten. It is amazing what incredible accuracy they achieve with a multitude of players."

Basically, what Dr. Long was saying was that you try for one hundred percent. But if you played a hundred percent every night, what would there be to look forward to? If you can consistently play at eighty percent or better, and you aim for the upper-ninety percentile, you will have really achieved success. That made me feel better. I don't know of any players that have gone through perfect seasons.

In my first year as principal trumpet in the Tulsa Philharmonic, our conductor said to us during our first rehearsal for the season, "I know that anyone can make a mistake. I consider two a habit." That can scare the hell out of you, because if you make your one mistake at the beginning, you have to worry about the whole rest of the season, or it can be a challenge based on the way you look at it. It is a daily chore to prove yourself, or it can be a challenge based on the way you look at it.

The old adage is true: the hardest thing isn't getting the job; it's proving day in and day out that you are worthy of it. This was something I often heard from my uncle Louis, and I tried to pass this on to my students as well.

Finally, one of the greatest lessons I ever learned about the psychology of playing, especially if you are a principal player, was the season in Dallas when we performed Ravel's "Piano Concerto in G," a piece written for a small orchestra of thirty-five musicians. At the end of the first movement is a famous little double-tongue solo, and you have to play this pattern eight times in a row. From the very first rehearsal, I struggled to get through it. I went home and after dinner I sat in the living room in front of the television with a cup mute and just kept playing the passage slowly over and over.

The next day at rehearsal, I managed to get four or five measures of the pattern before I lost it. That night at home, I put that cup mute in again and played the passage twenty or thirty times, a little faster. I did this the entire week up until our first concert on Sunday afternoon. When I left our apartment with my wife, I told her this was only the second time in my life that I was going to a concert knowing there was a passage that I could not play.

But at the concert, I absolutely nailed it to the wall. In fact, the orchestra turned around and shuffled their feet (the ultimate compliment), for they knew I had been struggling with it. Monday night I also played it flawlessly. I started to wonder what had happened. I finally figured it out, and it was a revelation: the fact that I had practiced it every night, increasing the tempo ever so slightly, until I was at the proper tempo by the night of the concert. When I had left on Sunday to perform, the final piece of the puzzle was my comment to my wife that I was leaving for a concert where I knew I couldn't play a particular passage. I was able to bring myself to a relaxed state to the degree where I could just go out there and do the best I could. The other element was by practicing it maybe two hundred times that week; I had prepared myself well to perform it.

It is also important, however, to realize when you encounter a passage that you know you don't have the capability to play and to step back for the sake of the music. I remember performing at the Playboy Club in Lake Geneva, Wisconsin with one of my idols, the great jazz vocalist Mel Torme. We had a four-hour rehearsal and were planning to break for dinner before doing the show. I had been playing third and fourth trumpet among some of Chicago's great trumpeters—John Howell, George Bean, and Russ Iverson.

Near the end of our rehearsal, the last tune was "Fascinating Rhythm," and Mel looked at me and said, "Ron, you play lead." I took the part and looked through it and, oh boy, right dead smack in the middle of the arrangement was a famous trumpet riff from the tune "Bugle Call Rag." Here the trumpet plays a solo that goes up to a high G above a high C, which I had not done in a very long time, and which I certainly found formidable after three-and-a-half hours of playing third and fourth trumpet.

We started the chart, without me having the chance to say anything, and when we got to my solo, I didn't play. Of course Mel stopped the band, looked at me, and asked what was the matter. I told him I couldn't play this and suggested that George Bean should do it; I knew George could perform it without even thinking about it. What is important about this experience is that I never had the least concern that the guys, or Mel Torme, would think less of me. My only thought was, let the person who can best play it, play it, so we get the maximum performance of the music. My first rule for our NIU Jazz Ensemble musicians was always to check your ego at the door. Our purpose, every moment, was to help each other make great music.

My son Christopher grasped the nature of performance at a very young age. When he was six, he heard me come home and practice, every night for two weeks, just four measures of the trumpet solo from Richard Strauss's "Das Burger als Edelmann." It was only a four-bar solo, but it began the third movement and was very exposed. Christopher and the rest of my children must have heard me play it at least twenty times a night, or between 240 and 300 times.

The afternoon of the concert, Christopher sat directly below the guest conductor, Anshel Brusilow, former concert-master of the Cleveland and Philadelphia orchestras. When it came time for my solo, I played it just as I had dreamed of playing it. I was so happy it had come off beautifully.

When we were backstage after the concert, my wife asked Christopher, "How did you like the concert?" "Fine," he replied. "How did you like dad's solo?" Christopher responded, "That was terrible." Why? "Because Daddy practiced that so many times and he only got to play it once." Is there a better description of a performer's life? Do we not practice and practice, rehearse and rehearse, and then have that one shot... that one chance to do it? You are on the spot, and it is only because of preparation, correct practice, and discipline that you possess the confidence to walk out on stage and feel there is no way in the world you are going to make a mistake.

The human mind plays such an incredible part in everything we do. If we put in the required, disciplined practice and then simply relax, it will come if it is within your playing capabilities, which it usually is. Let the mind relax and the fingers and tongue will take care of business.

STAYING IN THE GAME:
MY CAREER AS AN UMPIRE

Baseball has always been in my blood, and when my playing days were over I couldn't bear to give it up. Umpiring proved to be my way to stay in the game, and it blossomed into a kind of second career during my years at NIU.

I began my umpiring career after moving to Sycamore in June 1969 and contacting Ed Eggleston, the commissioner of little league baseball there. I told Ed I was new in town, had no kids of my own in little league, but that I would like to do some umpiring. Ed was shocked that someone would volunteer to do this. He set me up to coach two A league teams of nine- and ten-year-olds at Southeast School. He apologized because the two managers had the reputation of being umpire-baiters, and he was sorry to send me into the lion's den so quickly, but I told him not to worry and that I could handle the situation.

A few minutes before the game started, I called both managers up to home plate and introduced myself, telling them I had no children playing in the league. I also told them very emphatically that if I heard one word I didn't like, they would be watching the game from their car. I then turned and began to clean off home plate, leaving them with their mouths wide open. We never had a problem after that. What is so ironic is that one of those managers, Al Mirotznik, later became one of my closest and dearest friends.

I went on to umpire for twenty-two consecutive years and still think of those first few years in A league as the most fun, the most enjoyable times during my career as an umpire. Throughout, I used my sense of humor, successfully avoiding a lot of potentially hostile situations.

The one I remember most vividly was a night game in Genoa for the American Legion. I was behind the plate and some woman in the stands was giving me crap on every pitch. I let her go on for one or two innings, and then as the teams were changing sides I walked up into the stands and sat down right next to her. Everyone fell silent, until finally the woman looked at me as said, "What are you doing here?" I told her,

"Well, it has become very obvious that it's much easier to umpire from here than from where I'm at."

Another story that comes to mind was the time I umpired a game at NIU in mid April when the temperature was in the thirties. I was on the bases that day, as NIU faced the NAIA champions from Lewis University. The pitcher from Lewis committed the most infinitesimal balk I had ever seen, but I didn't react quickly enough, and NIU started to shout "Balk!" The unwritten rule was that I couldn't call the balk without seeming like I had been intimidated. At this point my good friend and NIU coach Walt Owens charged out to second base, stuck his face in mine, and shouted, "Didn't he balk?" "Yeah," I answered, "and I really blew the shit out of it!" Walt started to laugh, and when he got back to the dugout I could see the whole team huddled around him trying to find out what was so funny.

I finished my career in 1991, having gone from nine- and ten-year-olds in A league to college and semi-professional baseball. I loved every moment, but I was most thrilled in those early years to drive up to Southeast School and see four teams running toward my car, hollering "Are you doing our game tonight?"

It always moves me to hear from kids I've worked with, and one of my favorite letters came from a boy whom I had umpired when he was a catcher at DeKalb High School. I'm including his letter here, which highlights my signature umpire outfit of purple socks.

Perhaps my only frustration during my happy years behind the plate was that often too few parents would give their time to support the league. I was so concerned about this that when I served as commissioner of the Sycamore Little League, I wrote the letter which also follows to the DeKalb Daily Chronicle, imploring parents to step up to the plate. I hope very much that this lack of parental involvement is no longer an issue.

9 May 1997

Dear Ron,

*Well Sir, it's 4:30 in the morning and I could not sleep.
So it is with a certain degree of providence that I decided to flip on the TV and see a short news item on CLTV
regarding your retirement. Now I am not going to sing
the praises of an outstanding musician and teacher of
jazz as one expect and that you surely deserve. You see
you touched my life only briefly—as an umpire who
wore purple socks.*

*You probably don't remember a kid named Jim Rich way
back when . . . but I have never forgotten you. I was
a rather sullen youth who had the pleasure of playing
baseball in DeKalb during the years of Rip Collins and
Denny Pickett. It is a shame that not until one stares
40 in the face that one realizes the importance of all
the people that may cross your path in life and the roles
they play.*

*You see, I was a catcher who loved the game of base-
ball. And I remember a day when I looked up from the
bench to see a portly gentleman dusting off home before a summer game. Being young, brash, stupid and
opinionated (basically a catcher's resume), I chose to
pick on a most blatant infraction of baseball decorum
(even for the '70s). My umpire was wearing shorts with
purple socks!*

*You greeted me with a smile and asked my name and
proceeded to take control of the game. I had a habit
back then of never really arguing with my home plate
umpire. My method of disagreement revolved around
humiliation. I would frame a marginal pitch and hold it
. . . hold it, as if waiting for the umpire*

*to change his mind. When the strike call wouldn't come,
I'd drop my head—sometimes shake it—and slowly
raise up for a slow toss back to the pitcher.*

. . . You let me do that once . . .
*The next time I tried pulling that you said, "Jimmy, I
don't need your help embarrassing me out here. I do
enough of that on my own. Just catch the game, son."*

*Our next time together you pulled another trick. You
showed up for the game early, came into our dugout,
and proceeded to talk to us! What crust! An umpire
who didn't sit in his car until the last possible moment.
(By the way—same purple socks—I doubt you possess
two pair.) It seemed you did that every game.*

*Now for someone such as yourself, a world renowned
musician and teacher, these may seem small and insig-
nificant bits of life. Why then are they so vivid in my
memory? I believe it is because you recognize that in
all relationships, teacher and student, adult and child,
umpire and player, there needs to be a mutual respect
for the relationship to be pulled off.*

*So I thank you Ron. For showing a bunch of kids from
DeKalb that authority can be non-conventional
(in method and in fashion sense) and still possess a high
degree of caring and understanding.*

*I hope your retirement is long and happy. Good health
and God Bless.*

Sincerely,
JiM

Hey Dad, How Come?

(Editor's Note: The following letter was written, according to the author, "after some 150 phone calls trying to get parents to umpire Little League just two hours a week.")

Editor: Hey dad, how come you and mom used to peek in at me every few minutes after you brought me home from the hospital, but I couldn't ever get you to watch me at Little League? Gosh, dad, that sure would have meant a lot to me.

Hey dad, how come you were so anxious for me to join the Boy Scouts? I thought you would make at least one over-night with us. Sure was lonely out there, even with all the other dads.

Hey dad, how come you and mom were always saying, "We gotta do it for the kids," but when I asked you to sit down with me and look at my schoolwork you just couldn't give up that TV?

Hey dad, how come you always told mom, "our kids are gonna have MORE than we did," and then you couldn't hardly ever find the time to enjoy all that "MORE" stuff with me?

Hey dad, how come you and mom were always whispering and never told me what could happen when you do that with a girl?

Hey dad, how come you and mom thought birthday presents and Christmas presents and all the other nice things you bought me are all you need to say, I love you, I understand you, I respect your rights as an individual?

Hey dad, how come you and mom said you devoted your lives to making me happy and secure? Didn't you know room and board are just a small part of happiness and security?

Hey dad, how come you and mom didn't go to that PTA meeting when that nice sheriff was telling us what to watch out for with drugs and narcotics? Maybe I wouldn't have been so curious if you would have just talked to me about it.

Hey dad, how come you and mom were so proud when I was accepted at the university, and the first time I tried to talk to you about "change" you tuned me out? I just wanted to hear what you and mom thought; I never wanted to argue.

Hey dad, how come . . .
"Sorry, son, time's up."

Just one more minute, officer, please? Hey dad, how come it took a place like this for me to finally hear you say, "I love you, son!" It's too late dad.

Hey dad, how come it's too late?

Ron Modell, Commissioner
Sycamore Little League

LEON BREEDEN, THE DEAN OF COLLEGE JAZZ,
DEAR FRIEND AND MENTOR

NICOLA RESCIGNO,
ONE OF MY TWO GREATEST MUSICAL INSPIRATIONS.
THE PERFECT CONDUCTOR

KATHY MEETING TONY BENNETT,
WHO GAVE ME ONE OF MY GREATEST MUSICAL EXPERIENCES

MEL TORME,
ONE OF MY 3 IDOLS, WORKING TOGETHER AT THE
PLAYBOY CLUB IN LAKE GENEVA, WI, 1980

TIMOFEI DOKSHIZER & RON AT NIU,
CLINICING AND PERFORMING, 1978

DINNER I COOKED FOR
JOAN SCHILKE, RAYA GARBOUSOVA, AND TIMOFEI

INTRODUCING TIMOFEI TO VENICE BEACH, CA
WITH MY COUSIN EMIL DAVIDSON

MISTISLAV ROSTROPOVICH "SLAVA" RECEIVING HIS
HONORARY DOCTORATE AT NIU, 1990

QUINCY & I CONDUCTING IN GSTAAD, SWITZERLAND, 1997

"Q" VISITING US IN BRADENTON, FL, 2007

**Lew Soloff, Me, Vinnie DiMartino, Pat Harbison
Trumpet Section for ITG Premiere of
five episodes with "Doc"**

**President William Monat & I accepting
2 Chicago Emmys for
Vern Spevak and Louis Bellson**

Tito Puente 1992

"Tito" Puente, "El Rey" the King of Latin music

Cuban Pete
1st meeting in 48 years in chicago 'Penguino"

VIENNA, PRISON PERFORMANCE,
500 GUYS YELLING "YEAH BABY"

TWO OF THE MOST DEAR PEOPLE TO ME
MARYE AND WILBUR RAND
BUS DRIVER "EXTRADORDINAIRE" FOR 18 YEARS

RENOLD SCHILKE, MASTER CRAFTSMAN

BUD AND MAYNARD - TWO OF THE GIANTS OF BRASS

NIU JAZZ ENSEMBLE 1970-71
"THIS COULD BE THE START OF SOMETHING BIG

**1960-DALLAS SYMPHONY BRASS QUINTET -
VINCENZO VANNI, ARTHUR LEWIS, HAROLD YELTON,
RED BROMFIELD & ME**

**LES MCCURDY,
THE MAN WHO LAUNCHED MY THIRD CAREER**

PHIL COLLINS WITH THE NIU ALUMNI HORNS, 1998

SPEVAKS, KATZS, MODELLS, BETTCHERS
30 YEARS OF PURE JOY

VERY SPECIAL PEOPLE—AS GOOD AS IT GETS

Not long ago my wife Kathy posed this question to me: "When did you first realize what an incredibly interesting life you have led?"

Her question triggered a series of flashbacks, and I instantly thought of the many great performers, of all kinds, who truly touched my life. I would like to take some time here to share my experiences with some of these greats.

****

Timofei Dokshizer

For thirty-two years, Timofei Dokshizer served as the principal trumpet at the Bolshoi Theater in Moscow, where he was also revered as the greatest trumpet teacher in Russia. Because of his incredible stature, he was restricted, like other great musicians, in his movements outside the Soviet Union. Dokshizer was well aware of the surveillance that shadowed him—whenever my Uncle Louie dropped him off in New York City, he always did so several blocks from his hotel, at Timofei's request.

Although he was a superstar in the Soviet Union and throughout Europe, Timofei's recordings were not available in the United States, and for many years he was relatively unknown here. That all changed in 1965, when my uncle Louie, then teaching at Indiana University, met him following a concert there. It was Louie's custom to always invite the trumpet section of any visiting orchestra to his home for food and drink, so Timofei came for a late dinner. Later, my uncle played some old Cleveland Orchestra recordings for him. Although by now it was one in the morning, Timofei took out his trumpet and played for my uncle Louie.

Early the next morning my uncle called me. "Ronnie," he said simply, "last night I heard God play the trumpet."

This marked the start of what would become a close relationship between the Davidson-Modell family and Timofei Dokshizer. My uncle felt Dokshizer's genius so intensely that he partnered with his friend

James Stagliano principal French horn with the Boston Symphony, to produce a record album highlighting Timofei's performances. Their intent was not to make money, but to introduce Timofei Dokshizer to American music lovers. The albums were distributed to classical radio stations all over the country and played for their audiences. The response was tremendous—switchboards at radio stations lighting up like Christmas trees, all with the question, "Who is this playing?" Timofei always called my uncle Louie his "Christopher Columbus," the man who helped America discover him.

Having had the good fortune to work with the greatest artists in the worlds of opera, symphony, and jazz, I would single out Timofei Dokshizer as the greatest musician I ever heard. His greatest gift was his ability to find things in the music that none of us had ever dreamed possible. There was no technical challenge that Tima could not overcome, which gave him an incredible freedom to express himself in a way that touched the very core of his listeners.

In my last season with the Dallas Symphony, our final concert featured a solo by one of Timofei's oldest and closest friends, the great Russian cellist Mistislav Rostropovich. During a rehearsal break, I asked "Slava," as he was known, if he knew my friend Timofei. He responded in that deep Russian voice of his: "When I conduct Bolshoi, if no Timofei, no conduct." I asked the Maestro if I could send with him music, tape recordings, anything else that I knew Timofei could not purchase or acquire in the Soviet Union, and he kindly agreed to take these materials back to him.

The longest period of time that Tima was allowed to tour the United States came in 1977: fifteen days, at nine universities, much of which I spent with him. His appearance that year at NIU with its wind ensemble was one of the most astounding performances the university had ever hosted. Every one of Boutell Auditorium's 798 seats was taken. With the exception of myself, no one in the audience knew Dokshizer's reputation, yet when he came on stage to perform the audience gave him a standing ovation before he even played a note. Timofei had such a presence that whenever he entered any room, everyone immediately recognized that this was someone very important.

We wrote to each other for forty years and always spent as much time together as we could whenever he was in the States. Despite his limited English, we had no problem communicating, as Timofei proved one morning when we were driving together on Chicago's Lake Shore Drive after his concert at Northwestern University. We rounded a curve and he noticed the building with the two rabbit ears on it, looked at me, and said "Playboy!" Timofei marveled at American gadgets, like the lawn sprinkler he saw on a walk in Evanston that moved in an arc back and forth: "fantastic!" With the help of my friend Joan Schilke, we found one of those sprinklers he admired and sent it to Timofei in Russia, wrapped up in an old bassoon case.

If you have never heard Timofei Dokshizer play, the recording I would recommend would be George Gershwin's "Rhapsody in Blue," which he rearranged for trumpet and orchestra. I myself performed that piece on many occasions with American piano soloists who did not come as near to capturing its jazz flavor as did this great Russian.

Although Timofei and Slava had been close friends and colleagues in the Soviet Union, they lost touch with each other when Rostropovich defected to the United States. So when Timofei was performing at the University of Illinois, I called Slava at his New York apartment and gave him the number of Timofei's hotel room. One hour later I received a call from Timofei, who told me with great emotion, "Ich liebe dich; I love you." I loved this man beyond words. His music-making inspired millions of people during his lifetime.

The following are some of the most precious words he ever wrote to me, after hearing some recordings I sent him:

I have listened to your recordings of past years and your playing is simply stunning. What a great musician you are.

Embraces,
Timofei Dokshizer

Quincy Jones

The NIU Jazz Ensemble received a tremendous honor in 1996, when an invitation arrived from Claude Nobs, head of the Montreux Jazz Festival in Montreux, Switzerland. He asked if we would be available for a concert in July celebrating fifty years of the music of Quincy Jones. The plan was to feature artists like Phil Collins, Chaka Khan, Patti Austin, and David Sanborn, as well as a host of all-star jazz musicians. I responded with a resounding, "Yes!"

Before arriving in Montreux, the jazz ensemble first performed a series of six concerts all over Switzerland, leaving the last four days for the jazz festival. We arrived in Montreux on a Tuesday morning, ready to rehearse with Quincy from 1 pm to seven at night. The ensemble students were on such a high as they contemplated working with Quincy and the other artists—they reminded me of a quarterback at the beginning of a football game who takes an entire quarter to settle himself down. When I called Quincy at his hotel before our rehearsal and introduced myself, I asked if our band could play two of our numbers before getting into his music, thinking this would help settle my kids down. I also wanted Quincy to be able to hear our sensational vocalist, Stephanie Knox.

The first time Quincy heard the NIU Jazz Ensemble was one of the most thrilling moments of my career. As the band played its two charts, Quincy squeezed my hand a number of times, whenever the band did something incredible, whether dynamically or musicallyHe was so knocked out by Stephanie's voice that he invited her to join the vocal group he had brought from Cuba.

It was both exhausting and exhilarating to work with one of the giants in the history of the music industry. We had a six-hour rehearsal on Tuesday, a seven-hour rehearsal on Wednesday, a nine-hour rehearsal on Thursday, and then the ensemble took the stage from ten thirty in the morning on Friday until one in the morning on Saturday. There i not one student that would give up or forget any moment of time spen with Quincy Jones. We were at our very best: the great woodwind specialist, my friend Gary Foster, remarked to me after viewing a video c our concert, "There is not another band on this planet that could have played any better than your band performed that night."

When Quincy gifted me with his autobiography, this was his inscription:

> *I feel so blessed having you in my life—and most importantly, deep in my heart. I cannot tell you how much I've been looking forward to seeing you again. You da man, Ron! I cherish our memories with so much joy.*
>
> *In friendship and brotherhood,*
> *Quincy Jones*

Phil Collins

In 1997, after a full day of teaching at NIU, I came home and flipped on my home answering machine, to hear Quincy Jones's voice saying, "Ronnie! Where is your ass? I need you to call me as soon as you can: Phil Collins wants you to put together a big band for a two-month world tour!" I was elated: here was Phil Collins, one of the all-time idols of pop music, asking me to help fulfill a dream he had had for thirty-two years.

Phil's dream had begun in 1966, while he was drummer for the band Genesis and when he first heard the Count Basie Orchestra and the drummer phenom Buddy Rich. Phil vowed that some day he would do a world tour in which he would feature himself on the drums, not vocals, performing his greatest hits rearranged for big band. And now he was turning to me to make it a reality.

To achieve a big band sound, Phil asked me to hire five saxes, three trumpets, and three trombones. The best music arrangers in Los Angeles were brought in to tailor his music, so that each night on tour his audiences could hear a sampling of the signature sounds of the greatest big bands in our history. These include Count Basie, Stan Kenton and others.

I went through many years of rosters of former members of the NIU Jazz Ensemble, and chose musicians who were not only great players, but who also possessed the personality and temperament to live, work, and play together intensely for two months. The group that came together was almost indescribable in its ability night after night to hold to the highest standard, the art of music making. David Crosby, of Crosby, Stills and Nash, probably said it best when he remarked, "I've heard all the bands—Kenton, Woody, Buddy Rich, and this is the best big band of all."

We toured for two months, the first month in the U.S. and the second at Europe's greatest summer jazz festivals. Phil Collins and everyone connected with him, especially the Vine Street Horns, and his great rhythm section, made it memorable. On the night we played in

Copenhagen, I looked to my left and there was Tony Bennett sketching me. We had a wonderful reunion, having played together in the mid-1960s at the Statler Hilton Hotel in Dallas. When we performed at the Hague in the Netherlands, my former student Al Hood came over to me backstage and said, "Look who's come to see us tonight." It was Earth Wind and Fire. Ten minutes later, another student asked, "Can you believe who's here tonight to see us?" It was Tower of Power. Fifteen minutes later, another student exclaimed, "Cubanissimo has just come in!" We topped that in Paris, when Phil knocked on our door an hour before our concert to ask us to come out: "The Rolling Stones would like to meet you."

Phil Collins is an extraordinary musician, composer, outstanding big band drummer, and incredible human being. It was such a joy to be with him every day on that memorable tour and to share with him some of the greatest musical and personal moments of my life. All of us were on such a musical high that at the end of each concert, we were already looking forward to our next chance to play together.

I was very touched by this note tucked inside the case containing a very expensive Swiss watch:

Thanks for the "dream." Till next time!
Take care, Luv, Phil

Dizzy Gillespie

Trumpeter Dizzy Gillespie was a monumental figure in the history and world of jazz. I started working with Dizzy back in April 1977, when I invited him to come and do a four-day tour with the NIU Jazz Ensemble, I brought him back the following January to do an eleven-day tour.

Traveling with Dizzy for eleven days on our bus, piloted by our driver Wilbur Rand, was a real adventure for both Wilbur and me. Wilbur heroically assumed the task of making sure that Dizzy was always on time, a difficult responsibility. My assignment was equally challenging—to make sure Dizzy's unorthodox smoking habits during our tour were not visible to anyone. Dizzy was irrepressible in so many ways. He also endeared himself on tour with the food he prepared using his food-contraption, "La Machine." At everyplace we stayed, Dizzy kept his hotel room door open, inviting anyone who walked by to come in and sample the healthy soups and foods he was constantly creating.

The way Dizzy worked with young musicians was something to see. As a great percussionist himself, he gave wonderful advice to young drummers. Whatever high school we visited, Dizzy's first move was always to immediately go up to the drummer and deliver this classic advice: "I don't care what you do, as long as everybody knows where 'one' is." He was making the larger point that in a big band, the drummer is the one responsible for keeping nineteen other musicians together, and also serves as the driving force for the rest of the band.

Dizzy's sense of humor was legendary, as seen in this very funny line he gave me to deliver at an NIU luncheon for the parents of our African-American students. Deacon Davis, my NIU colleague who ran our CHANCE program, asked me to furnish the luncheon with a jazz combo and to make a few remarks. I was scratching my head, wondering what I would say. Dizzy nailed it. I told him of my plight, and he immediately remembered how the great mini-series "Roots" had just transfixed the nation. So I stood up and said, "Good afternoon, ladies and gentlemen, and welcome to the campus of Northern Illinois University. We are delighted that you can be here, but I am afraid I am the bearer of some very bad news. They've just found out that Alex Haley was adopted!" (Thank you, Dizzy!)

I also remember a phone call I received from him at one in the morning. Being a night owl, I don't think I was asleep, but I certainly wondered who could be calling at that time. I instantly recognized Dizzy's voice, commanding me, "Ron, get a piece of music paper and write down this rhythm!" So I did, and then he demanded, "Now, sing it to me!" It was a fairly complex rhythm, and I took a minute to look it over before I sang it back to him. He started laughing with that wonderful laugh of his, exclaiming "I told Moody!" Of course, he was talking about the great James Moody. "Moody and I just got back from Israel, and we heard this Jewish guy playin' this rhythm, and I told Moody, 'This is the way it should go' but Moody says no, it's not like that. So I called you. We just got back tonight, and I called you cause you were the first Jew we could think of. I knew you would know how it really went!" In addition to his being an iconic musician, one of the founding fathers of bebop jazz, and significant composer, Dizzy had an unparalled sense of humor, and was an incredible human being, deservedly loved by all.

James Moody

My friend Quincy Jones has said on many occasions, "I would not have wanted to live in any other time period than the one I am living in, because we have had Ella, and Sarah, and Duke, and Count, and people like Moody." Of course he meant the incomparable James Moody, one of the greatest saxophonists and jazz flutists of our time.

Moody burst upon the jazz world in the 1940s, yet even in the 1980s when he toured with our NIU Jazz Ensemble, he was still eager to learn. After each concert, back on the bus, Moody would be sitting with the sax section, questioning them intently about their improvisations that night. To be asked for advice by one of the greatest jazz musicians of our time gave our students a sense of validation that was priceless.

He was like a brother to me, in the sense that we could share confidences that perhaps only brothers would. I met him when he was going through a new period in his life, so I got him at a good time.

Years ago, on a Sunday afternoon, I made the sixty-mile drive into Chicago from DeKalb because I knew Moody was appearing at the Jazz Showcase, Joe Segal's old place at the Blackstone Hotel, where the NIU Jazz Ensemble had performed many times. I planned to hear him play and then catch up with him over dinner. Moody's Sunday afternoon set ran from four to five-thirty, but little did we know, inside of the windowless club, that a major snowstorm had blanketed Chicago. By the time the set was over, we were confined to the Blackstone's coffee shop for our dinner. I called my wife Kathy to tell her it was impossible to drive, so I'd be bunking down with Moody in his room at the Blackstone.

I obviously had no pajamas. When I undressed down to my underwear, there was Moody, standing next to me and getting ready to step out of his boxer shorts to put on his pajamas. He looked at me and delivered a classic remark: "Ron, you know all that shit they tell you about black guys? It ain't true!" A great laugh, at a perfectly timed remark. I loved James Moody.

These are a few of the liner notes Moody wrote for the NIU jazz ensemble album, "Live at Montreux:"

The respect that they had for one another was just fantastic, and I could see the reason why all of the students were such wonderful people, wonderful ladies and gentlemen, and Ron Modell was like a father to them, a friend to them, and with students feeling that way towards each other, the music can't help but get better and better.

Maynard Ferguson

I had known jazz trumpeter Maynard Ferguson since the mid-1950s, first meeting him in Tulsa where he was touring along with Dave Brubeck's quartet and a wonderful vocal jazz group, Lambert, Hendricks, and Ross. This was a truly memorable encounter. I remember vividly how well his band performed my favorite big band chart of all times, Slide Hampton's great "Framework for the Blues," a cut from their album "A Message from Newport," What a great album: Bill Chase on lead trumpet, Jake Hanna on drums, Frank Strazzeri on tenor, Jimmie Ford on Alto, Harry Hall and Bob Summers in the trumpet section.

Maynard gave a wonderful concert with the NIU jazz ensemble in September 1986, but his most memorable performance in northern Illinois came when he called me out of the blue in the early 70's, to say he had a cancellation in our area. "I would give anything," he said, "just to make our expenses and not have a lost day. Can you get me a gig some place?" I called my friend Rod Thomas, the band director at Genoa-Kingston High School, and delivered the good news: "We can have Maynard Ferguson and his band for $1500!" This was a band that was then getting about seven thousand dollars a night. In the high school gymnasium in this town of three thousand, we drew an audience of 1500 people. Ferguson was just breaking in a new album that he had recently recorded, and before the concert we talked in his dressing room about "Conquistador," one of its cuts. He told me that there was a place on it where all four trumpets came out and each did an unaccompanied cadenza. "I am going to call you, Ron, to come up and play." "Maynard,' I had to tell him, "you know I can't improvise. It would be terribly embarrassing for me. All my students were here; all the kids from the area know me."

So of course I nearly died when we got to that tune and Maynard Ferguson told the audience, "You know, there's a guy here who has been bugging me for years to play with my band, so I'm going to give him that chance right now—if you would help me, folks, let's get Ron Modell up here to help me with our new recording of "Conquistador.""

What do you do then? I came up on the stage, Maynard handed me his trumpet, and then each of the other trumpet players came out and played incredible, Spanish-style cadenzas. And then it was my turn. I turned to the drummer, the great Peter Erskine, and said, "I'm going to do a little thing from 'Capriccio Español,' so all I need is a snare drum roll—and after the drum roll, I want you to go into the Jewish beat that we use on that great classic, "Hava Nagila."

I played my little Spanish thing, and the audience loved it, yelling "Ole!" at the finish. Then one of my students in the ensemble, Dave Carpenter, called out "Oy vey!" and the place broke up. I turned to Peter and he started up that Jewish rhythm, going right into the chorus of "Hava Nagila." After I finished the first chorus, the rest of the band joined in and played raucously. It was a wonderful evening, and I was happy to have gotten myself out of improvising by using a little guile and, as I have done all my life, a little humor.

When Maynard came to NIU in 1972, he was engaged in a very hectic schedule. One night I drove him back to DeKalb after listening to him play in Milwaukee, and we ended up at three in the morning having a bite at a little coffee shop on Lincoln Highway before turning in at four. And then four hours later, at eight in the morning, we were having breakfast together at the cafeteria in the Holmes Student Center, while I interviewed Maynard for my uncle Louis Davidson's book, *Trumpet Profiles*.

At ten, he gave his first clinic, listening to my student Ron Friedman's jazz lab band. Shortly before eleven, I told Maynard, "You've got an hour off now, and I know you haven't slept much—can I run you back to your room so you can grab a quick nap? Or you could also hear our faculty brass quintet rehearse, a really wonderful piece by a composer named Dahl." Maynard said he'd like to sit in on the rehearsal.

So picture me sitting on the outside of the quintet, the other trumpet player facing me, and Maynard sitting next to me on my right. We started rehearsing the first movement, and at one point my trumpet part called for me to play fourth spaced E *pianissimo*, written as two p's, very softly, holding it for twelve counts. I had really great chops that day, and when I played the *pianissimo*, it was more like three or four p's, and the note seemed to vibrate all over the room. When I was just about to count eight, Maynard leaned over and spoke into my right ear: "Why don't you go fuck yourself?" Of course, that was the end of the rehearsal. Everybody broke up! Maynard Ferguson had never heard anybody play that softly before, nor had he ever been asked in any of his work to play that softly. I, in turn, would have given anything to have one experience of playing a solo or playing in a section the way that Maynard used to. He was one in a million.

This is an excerpt from a letter after he had listened to the latest recording of the NIU Jazz Ensemble:

> *My personal applause to you as a music educator, great bandleader, friend, blues singer, and screech trumpet player supreme!*
>
> *Maynard*

Red Rodney

Red Rodney, the legendary be-bop trumpeter who played for years with Charlie Parker (one of the two innovators of be-bop, and considered the greatest alto saxist of his time), came to Northern Illinois University in January 1992 to be a soloist and clinician with the jazz ensemble. It was a new experience for Red, the first time he had ever toured with a college band.

"Albino Red," as he was known in jazz circles, got his nickname from the persona he had been forced to assume when touring in the south with Charlie Parker. During the 1940s and 50s, southern towns would not permit groups that mixed the races to perform or even to stay in all-black hotels there. Red came from a white Jewish family in Philadelphia, but to trick southern authorities he pretended to be an African-American albino.

During his tour with us, Red told me that on his very first professional tour, with the Jimmy Dorsey Orchestra, they had played one week in Peoria. Only sixteen years old, making ninety dollars a week back in the 1940s, he had spent his entire week's wages at "Big Al's," a gentlemen's club right next to the famous Pere Marquette Hotel.

I called my friend Mary Jo Papich and told her I wanted to play a practical joke on Red, who was by now my wonderful new friend. A few days later, as our bus driver Wilbur drove us through downtown Peoria, we passed by the spot where "Big Al's" had stood. To the amazement and delight of our guest artist, a huge banner there read "Welcome back Red!"

At the conclusion of our tour, Red autographed a photo to the jazz ensemble for our yearly album: *"Thank you for one of the greatest weeks I've ever had."* Sadly, a year later he called to tell me he was battling cancer. But the very day I talked to him, he had received two phone calls. The first was from Clint Eastwood, calling to tell him to please come to Los Angeles for treatment and that he would cover all medical expenses. Eastwood had worked closely with Red when producing his film "Bird" based on the life of Charlie Parker. The second call was from President Bill Clinton himself. "I want to see you back at the White House, with your trumpet or without," the president told him, referring to Red's recent White House performance. He was absolutely thrilled that these two giants thought enough of him to call and "make his day."

Tito Puente

    Tito Puente was called "El Rey," a nickname that means "The King," and he was an icon in the field of Latin music. I first saw him perform at the Palladium in New York when I was playing there with Joe Cuba in the late 1950s. But I really didn't get to know him personally until the early 1990s, when I invited him to appear as soloist with the NIU jazz ensemble and to give a series of clinics and concerts in northern Illinois's heavily populated Latino areas of Elgin and Aurora.

    My intent was to introduce Tito Puente to a younger generation, who turned out to be absolutely thrilled to discover him and his music. At the same time, our evening concerts electrified their parents as well, connecting them with what was their own "root music"—to the point where some of them were moved to get up out of their seats and dance in the aisles. I don't think I ever heard a more exciting performer in my entire career.

    I was also introducing my students to *cojunto* music, or authentic Latin music, which they had never played before. They rose to the challenge and were soon playing music that was *rico, calienete, y sabroso*, or red, hot, and sensual. Tito couldn't get over how quickly the NIU jazz ensemble took to Latin music, but my years of playing with Latin bands had given me the tools and experience to prepare them. We were also helped by Tito's musical director, Jose Madera, and his great bongo player Johnny Rodriguez. Tito's visit gave our students the experience of a lifetime.

    Tito was the consummate musician, composer, bandleader, and happy-go-lucky human being. The last time I visited with him, I surprised him in Dallas, where he was appearing as soloist with the Dallas Symphony Orchestra. What a wonderful memory I have of walking into his dressing room following the concert and seeing him light up like a Christmas tree when he saw me. That visit is especially precious to me, for Tito died suddenly just two weeks later. I loved him like a brother.

    This was the inscription on a huge poster Tito gave me which portrayed him on the postage stamp of his native Puerto Rico:

Ron, beautiful friend, musician, and an inspirator to all in our Latin music!

Tito Puente
"El Rey"

Renold Schilke

Renold Schilke was renowned as one of the greatest craftsmen of trumpets. His horns were of the highest quality, hand-crafted one at a time at his factory on Wabash Avenue in Chicago. They were prized by great trumpet players who performed with them on stages all over the world.

In the forty years that I knew him, his initial response to my phone call was always the same: "Hello Ren, how are you?" "Turrible!" While he tried to give the impression of being a crusty old man, those of us who really knew him found a warm and gentle heart. I don't think we will ever know how many trumpets and mouthpieces he provided musicians, as well as the refuge of his home. Ren didn't like to work on instruments that had not been made in his factory, and whenever I would walk in with my Benge trumpet for some kind of repair, he would throw his arms up in the air and shout, "Why don't you put that thing in a museum where it belongs?"

One of the last times we met was at the International Trumpet Guild conference in Bloomington, Indiana. Ren was slated to give a lecture, and although he was usually not a very exciting lecturer, that night he delivered a superb presentation on the technical aspects of making brass instruments. I waited afterwards to tell him how wonderful I thought he had been, while four people from the audience were clustered around him. I decided to have some fun with this very serious man, so I approached the group and just as Ren looked up I exclaimed, "You don't know what the hell you're talking about!"

The people turned white, and Ren threw his arm up in the air and motioned to me, oh just go on. The next morning the first panel consisted of Charles Colin, my uncle Louis Davidson, and myself. I immediately took the microphone and made the following announcement: "If any of the four people are present this morning who witnessed my comment to Mr. Schilke last night, know that it was a joke. Thank you."

When Ren passed away, his daughter Joan asked me to speak at his memorial service. I cautioned her that my remarks would be humorous ones, which she said was precisely the reason she was asking me: "I don't want this service to be maudlin." With the greatest brass players in the world there to pay their respects, I told a story that I thought was quintessential Ren.

I had brought my horn in to Ren for a complete overhaul and asked to borrow a loaner while mine was being worked on. He came back with his own personal gold-plated Schilke B4, handed it to me, saying "Take care of my horn." Later that week, while performing a quintet concert with our NIU group for high school students, I put the trumpet down on my seat.

I got flustered when I realized I couldn't find the right music, and in my haste and confusion I sat down right on Ren Schilke's personal trumpet. My weight at that time was probably two hundred thirty pounds, and there is no way I can describe how that trumpet looked after I got up. Try to visualize one of those hot pretzels that you might buy.

I was, of course, beside myself. I ran to my office to call Phil Warship, the manager at the factory. I explained to Phil what had happened and offered him any amount of money to make the horn look like new. It took him several minutes to stop laughing, but he agreed, and one of my students who was heading into Chicago dropped it off for me. When I got it back, I was relieved to see it looked absolutely perfect. I returned it to Ren, thinking I had dodged the bullet.

Several years later, I called Ren to say my Eb trumpet was in need of an overhaul, and he told me to bring it to his home that evening. Ren lived in the woods near Wheaton, and as I approached his front door I could hear the growling of Anna, his big Doberman. Preferring to remain outside, I asked Ren if he could give me a loaner Eb trumpet. He stuck the horn out of the door, and as I walked off I suddenly heard him holler after me, "And don't sit on this one, or I'll tell Anna you're Jewish!"

I stopped dead in my tracks and asked him, "How did you know?" He had waited years for the perfect moment to tell me this. "I knew from the moment you put the horn in my hand that it had been damaged, right where the bell flares out. You could never hide this from me."

Ren Schilke is one of the three people who greet me every day of my life when I sit down at the desk in my study. On the wall hang together three decoupage portraits. They were crafted at my request by one of my former students. The portraits are of three important men in my life: Timofei Dokshizer, my uncle Louis Davidson, and Renold Schilke. Each portrait is inscribed with one word that I felt best describes them. For Timofei, it is "artistry"; for Uncle Louis, "vitality': and for Renold I chose "creativity."

Joe Paterno

One of my real heroes was the legendary football coach Joe Paterno. We were pen pals for thirty-five years. He made a strong impression on me, after I watched one of the greatest bowl games ever, when Penn State lost a heartbreaker to Bear Bryant's Alabama. At the post-game press conference, Coach Paterno was asked what the mood was like in his locker room, and he said that half his players had their heads down and the other half were in tears.

Coach said he had told his players to go immediately across to the Alabama locker room, shake the hand of every player, and tell them what a thrill it had been to play in that game with them. I was so moved by this that I sat right down and wrote him a letter, telling him how proud I was of him as a coach and as a great teacher.

To my delight, one week later I received my first letter from Joe Paterno, the beginning of what would be a long and cordial correspondence. I finally got to meet him in 1999, when NIU coach Joe Novak invited my wife Kathy and me to join the NIU team when they played their opener at Penn State. I called Coach Paterno, told him when we were arriving, and he invited us to his pre-game press conference on Friday afternoon.

As Kathy and I walked into the Nittany Lion Inn, she remarked that she had never seen me so nervous. I simply told her, "Honey, this is one of the great men that walks our earth." As we walked into the press conference, Joe spotted me, stopped the proceedings and announced "Here comes the real star." I was so shocked I looked around to see who he was talking about. What a way to finally meet my good friend in person.

At the post-game conference, Kathy noticed how Coach Paterno refused to belittle the NIU team, despite pressure to do so from the press corp. She also commented what a gentleman he was, always making her feel part of the conversation. Joe forecast a greatfuture for NIU in its first season with Joe Novak as head coach. His team forecast turned out to be right on target.

The last letter I wrote to him was when word of that terrible scandal first broke. I simply wrote, "I will love you forever." All of us who admired, respected, and loved Joe Paterno prayed that his knowledge of these despicable acts began when his quarterbacks coach reported to him in 2011. What a crushing blow it was to all of us to find out that he had known for many years and had helped in causing irreparable damage to many young people.

I want to make a musical analogy to Joe Paterno's life. A musician might perform a concerto of three thousand notes and play 2,999 of them perfectly. But if he misses badly on that last note, this is what the audience will remember. Until Coach Paterno somehow lost his way, in his life as a coach, teacher, mentor, and great friend to Penn State, he had played a perfect concerto. We must never lose sight of this.

This is an excerpt from one of the many letters we exchanged:

*You are providing a platform for so many young people
to show their talents and to test their creative abilities.*

Joe Paterno

Wilbur Rand

One of the most important people who contributed to the tremendous success of the NIU jazz ensemble was Wilbur Rand, godfather of NIU transportation and bus driver extraordinaire. He was absolutely indispensable, and for eighteen years we had hands-down the best bus driver in the country.

Whether driving on ice-covered roads or battling blizzards at forty below, he always got us there and back safely. Having driven an 18 wheeler earlier in his career, Wilbur knew all the back roads as well as the best breakfast spots.

Every student, every guest artist, all knew Wilbur was not only a skilled driver but also an integral part of our ensemble. On tour we always had to stick to a very strict schedule, and for some students this was a real challenge. Wilbur came up with the solution: we would give the students half of their per diem allowance on the first day of the tour, but reserve the option to deduct one dollar for every minute a student was late. Wilbur's other great idea was to take all the money we collected at the end of the tour and use it to throw the band a big pizza party. You can see that he obviously was not just the bus driver.

His greatest challenge came during our spring tour of 1981, when he drove us to New York City and had to battle Manhattan traffic for the first time in his life. Wilbur had quit smoking and just celebrated his three-month anniversary of being smoke-free, but by the time we reached our hotel and he had parked our bus at the New York Port Authority, you guessed it—he had broken down and bought cigarettes.

I got to show Wilbur my respect and deep affection for him when I asked him to share with my oldest son Scott, the honor of serving as best man at my marriage to Kathy.

Louis Bellson and Pearl Bailey

"The sweetest, kindest, and most gentle man that walks the earth: ladies and gentlemen, Mr. Louis Bellson:" that's how I introduced Louis Bellson to audiences for over twenty years. Everyone who ever met Louis loved and adored him.

He was without a doubt one of the all-time greatest drummers in our history. To listen and watch one of his extended drum solos was like watching a ballet dancer or a great concert artist. When Louis was behind the drums, the look on his face was as bright as the brightest star you've ever seen. He was also a significant composer, with his charts played by both big bands and symphony orchestras.

During my years at NIU, Louis toured with the jazz ensemble more than any other artist. He also donated more than $35,000 worth of music from his own library to the jazz ensemble, which was immensely helpful to our program. I nominated Louis to be awarded an honorary doctorate by NIU for his long-time support and generous contributions to the school of music, an award he received in 1985, where he delivered a moving speech about his life story and the importance of music education.

To say we were like brothers is an understatement. To commemorate our friendship, I gave Louis a gold disc to wear around his neck: on the front were the ten commandments in Hebrew, and on the back I had written, "between two men, no greater love exists."

I also came to know well Louis's magnificent wife, the incomparable Pearl Bailey, not only as a super-star but also as our special ambassador to the United Nations. My first meeting with Pearl came at a drum competition in Las Vegas, a contest sponsored by the Slingerland Drum Company, to find the most talented young drummer, aged seventeen or younger. Louis Bellson had won this same contest some fifty years earlier. Since NIU had a drummer competing and Louis was one of the judges, I was told understandably not to speak to him until the contest was over.

I ran into Louis and Pearl having breakfast at the Riviera Hotel, and after saying hello, Louis immediately got up and left. Pearl and I began to talk, and we instantly connected, launching into a conversation that would last for four hours before we moved to her hotel room to talk for another three.

What we discovered was that both of our families were struggling with a terrible problem that many families are plagued with— children who become dangerously involved with drugs. Our support for each other was sometimes expressed in our letters, one of which I'm enclosing here. It is worth reading by every child, both those who have gotten into drugs and others that are still struggling to take responsibility for their lives.

I am also enclosing a letter that deals with my own daughter's drug addiction, one I wrote after attending my first Narcotics Anonymous meeting at her invitation. I am very happy to report that my daughter's story ends happily, for she has been drug-free now for eleven years, while serving as a spokesperson for Narcotics Anonymous.

December 26, 1980

Dear, dear Ron,

I'm so glad you took the time to write to me. Tell your children they have responsibilities they must live up to—to be firm when you tell them and finally mean it.

If they are of age and just don't want to fit the program, then let them make a path that will not be easy to walk for themselves.

Tell them how much (as I do in lectures), "If they can't take directions at home, wait, oh wait, until they hit the streets."

Try believing the drugs will straighten you—well my dears, if you get high—you sure will have to get low someday—and that's a drag.

One thing no man can avoid is the looking in the mirror of self!!

It's tough to love your children and say, "Hey, where did I go wrong?" Weeeeellll my friend, at their age tell them to ask themselves, "Where are they going wrong?" Why are you supposed to owe them more than they owe you or themselves and visa-versa

This is only to say I've walked the same path as you. Louie walked slower on it, but Lawdy!!! Did he find out—and we left them to know it all—Brother are they learning—one is still battling humanity but Time Cures all (good and evil). Girls are tougher than boys to raise, but tell madam this is a female talking.

Bless you always and know in your heart you have done your best. It will somehow or other work out for all.

All love always,
Pearl

Reflections on Narcotics Anonymous, 2 September 2005,
Utica, New York

First and foremost, thank you for helping to bring back
to me and to all our family, one of our most treasured
possessions, my baby girl, Lisa.

I am seventy years old and have yet in my lifetime to
ever hold a marijuana cigarette. Was this because I
was sheltered or not exposed? Not at all! In my eighth
grade graduating class at P.S. 48 in the Bronx, of the
sixty-six boys in my class, at least twenty two had prison
records, and in addition, one had since been electrocut-
ed for murder.

Two major events in my life kept me from ever being
tempted. First, at age sixteen, I was bedded down for
six weeks with walking pneumonia. During that period
of being bedridden, I listened on the radio every day to
the first-ever broadcast of the drug hearings being held
in New York City. I heard kids from my neighborhood,
ages ten to twelve, who were already heroin addicts,
and their horror stories of what it is like to need a fix
and not be able to get one.

The physical and mental pain scared the shit out of me
to the point where I was frightened to death to even try
pot.

My second event was my career in music. Music has
been my high for over sixty years, and even though I
have been around drugs playing with some of the great
Latino bands in New York—Machito, Joe Cuba, and
Tito Puente—I could not be tempted. Lisa can tell you
that in the past five to seven years I have been closely
associated with Quincy Jones, Phil Collins, Patti Austin,
and Chaka Khan.

Once again, that is an environment where drugs are easily accessible. I never saw any of these people use drugs or get involved with alcohol, but believe me, it was there.

Between my music and my great fright, I have been blessed with a drug-free life. Hearing all of you share last night gives me great hope that with your love and support, and most important, "one day at a time," my baby girl is in a wonderful safe place, and my prayers have been answered. Thank you again.

Peace and love,
Ron

KATHY, LOVE OF MY LIFE

I met my beautiful wife Kathy at NIU's mixed bowling league in 1988. I had asked one of my female teammates if she knew of any single women who were really nice. She pointed a few lanes down from us, saying "I think Kathy Pavelick is a lovely person." I already knew some of Kathy's teammates, having gone over to exchange a few jokes with them.

A few days later, I called Kathy, then working at NIU's Provost's office, and asked if she would like to go bowling after work, have dinner, and then go see a movie. She agreed to the bowling and dinner, but told me she had a regular square dance class on Tuesday nights. We met at the Huskie Den, and I was doing great until all of a sudden, after releasing the ball, I felt something snap in my right middle finger. That was the end of my bowling for a month.

We went to dinner and found ourselves ordering almost the identical meal, right down to the salad dressing. After three more dates, I was off to New Jersey to spend Thanksgiving with my father, while Kathy went down to Springfield, Illinois to spend the holiday with her mother. While I was out shopping with my dad, my eyes settled on a beautiful winter sweater, and I instantly thought I have to buy that for Kathy for Christmas. I couldn't imagine we weren't going to keep seeing each other. What is so ironic is that, at the exact same time, Kathy was purchasing a winter sweater as a Christmas present for me.

After Thanksgiving, we started dating steadily, and by the new year we were a couple. At that point, both of us proclaimed that marriage was out of the question.

As we began to date, I was not at first aware that ten month prior Kathy had lost her twelve-year-old son, Brad, to a brain tumor Having six children of my own, I could not even begin to imagine wha she had been through in those last months of Brad's life. Where mos people hesitated to talk about Brad, I wanted to know all about him There were a lot of tears, a lot of holding each other, and it was durin those times that I could see what a wonderful mother Kathy was.

As we became closer and closer, I found a woman whose honesty I could trust one hundred percent of the time, someone who would always tell it like it was, so you knew where you stood all of the time. It's funny that both of us agree that if we had met thirty or forty years ago, we probably would not have made it as a couple. It is good when we can all learn from experience, and having Kathy in my life has made me happier in the past twenty-five years than I ever dreamed possible.

I am sure there is no greater grandma or step-mom than Kathy. There is not a minute during the day that she is not thinking about all of them. When I was umpiring, I could never manage more than two games a day, but she recently sat through four little league games to watch her grandsons. The joys of grand-parenting are like no others, and they can serve as a buffer sometimes in delicate situations.

We have enjoyed escaping the winters of Illinois for the past fifteen or twenty years at our home in Bradenton, Florida. I could go on and on about Kathy, but let me share with you one of the most daring things she ever did.

After the jazz ensemble performed at the Chicago Jazz Festival in 1992, Kathy asked me, "How can you be so relaxed and comfortable, standing and talking in front of thirty thousand people? I could never do that! I couldn't even speak in front of twenty people." This is why it was so amazing and astonishing when Kathy gave her first public speech at my retirement dinner in 1997 to a packed NIU Sky Room.

I had no idea she was scheduled to speak; the program had merely said "guest speaker." Hearing her words touched me as deeply as I have ever been touched in my life. I will let her words that follow speak for themselves.

Even though we love our family and cherish our friends, every week we hug and remind each other that, when all is said and done, "It's you and me."

Speech by Kathy Modell at tribute dinner given by IAJE students at Northern Illinois University, 8 April 1997.

You have heard about Ron Modell the musician, Ron the joke teller, co-worker, friend, etc. now let me tell you what he's REALLY like! Now he's getting nervous . . . You can guess, and a lot of you have seen how much fun Ron and I have together. Ron even makes washing dishes fun! I won't tell you how, but believe me, I've never had such a good time washing dishes. A lot of my friends have a plan for Ron when he retires. After listening to me talk about how he spoils me rotten, they want him to start a school for husbands (and they want to be the first to enroll their own husbands). In addition to all his other wonderful qualities, Ron is the kindest man I have ever known.

I met Ron at a time when I thought all the good things in my life were over. My twelve year old son, Brad, had died the previous year from a brain tumor. All you parents out there will know that losing a child is about the most devastating thing that can happen to you I was in bad shape emotionally I was "existing." Then I met Ron. Talk about being in the right place at the right time. When I would get upset about missing Brad, Ron would not be uncomfortable or embarrassed; he would not change the subject or tell me not to cry as so many people would. He encouraged me to talk, and he would ask questions about Brad, or he would just hold me while I sobbed. Ron helped me bear all the pain and sorrow—he treated me with tenderness and understanding and helped me heal a broken heart. I started looking forward to life instead of dreading it.

When Ron and I got married (after a whirlwind courtship of over four years neither of us was EVER going to get married again), this man who is completely at home on stage in front of thousands of people, had to take a tranquilizer. He was as stiff as a board.

*When Cheryl Porter and Tony Boyd were singing
OUR song, Ron wouldn't look at me. I kept squeezing
his hand and wanting to gaze into his eyes. He still
wouldn't look at me his hand was probably bruised, I
squeezed it so hard. He told me later he was afraid if
he looked at me he would break down. At the reception,
Ron was finally able to relax, and we had a ball. And
life gets better every day that I'm married to this sweet,
sentimental guy.*

*You've probably heard a lot of mother-in-law jokes from
Ron, none of them complimentary, right? Well, Ron is
so crazy about my mom (and the feeling is mutual); he
is always suggesting she be with us for weekends, vaca-
tions, etc. Last summer, when we were going to Switzerland, he wanted to take her too. When we told her she
was going on the trip, she let out this loud whoop and so
excited she couldn't sleep that night. He's also a great
step-father to my son Brian. Brian has the greatest
respect and admiration for Ron also likes his jokes. And
Ron treats Brian the same as he does his own sons—
with love and encouragement (and a sense of humor).*

*Everyone who knows Ron knows that he is one of the
hardest people to buy gifts for. He gets greater pleasure
from giving to others, so a present to him is OK, but his
greatest joy comes from making other people happy. My
mom says she has to be careful about what she wishes
for, because she turns around and there it is before she
knows it, Ron has gotten it for her.*

*One summer I was on a weekend in Wisconsin on an
antiquing trip with several of my friends I saw a beautiful antique necklace but decided not to spend the money.
That Christmas (like five months later) I opened this
gift from Ron, and there was the necklace. My friend,
Doris, had told Ron how much I liked the necklace, so*

*he got on the phone, traced down the owner of the
store, and had her send the necklace. He managed to
keep that secret all those months. He loves to surprise
people. Ron thinks of things to do that no one would
ever think of. I planted a blue spruce evergreen in
my churchyard as a memorial to my son. He died on
December 8, so each year on December 8 we have a
memorial service and light Brad's tree with little white
lights. It stays lit throughout the holidays and certainly
brightens my Christmas. But Ron was not content with
my being uplifted only during the holidays. One spring
day during lunch, I could tell something was on Ron's
mind. He eventually told me that he had a surprise for
me (Ron is full of surprises), but I wouldn't get it until
that night. So after work, I, of course, couldn't wait for
the surprise. But Ron wanted to go out and grab something to eat first (more suspense, more waiting).*

*When we got home, he made me sit on the couch with
my eyes closed. When I opened them, there was this
large painting faced away from me so I couldn't see the
picture, but I could see what was written on the back.
It said, "In memory of Brad." He turned the frame
around, and there was a painting of Brad standing in
the snow with his sled looking at "his" tree. When I
looked more closely, Brad had wings and a halo. Need-
less to say, I cried not only because of the memories, but
because this sweet man had thought to do such a beautiful, caring thing. He wanted me to enjoy the beauty of
Brad's tree, not just at Christmas, but all year long.*

*I like the word "precious" a word used to describe
something so rare and valuable that you can't even put
a price on it that's how I feel about this man. But he is
truly amazed when I tell him how special he is. Because
his kindness and generosity come so naturally to him, it
doesn't seem unusual or special to him, it's just the way
he is.*

Ron is the love of my life, the coach who encourages and brings out the best in me, the gentle father I never had, a great playmate when we want to have fun, my life-long partner in good times and bad, and most of all, my very, very best friend.

LIFE AFTER NORTHERN ILLINOIS UNIVERSITY:
RICHES AND REWARDS

My career at NIU propelled me into a new chapter of my life that I could never call "retirement." The reputation of NIU's jazz ensemble, both nationally and internationally, allowed me to pursue my fondest wish—to continue working with high school and college students, sharing both my musical knowledge and life experience. I also have enjoyed the surprise of a new career as a stand-up comic.

When I look back at my life and reflect, it is heartwarming to relive the wonderful blessings that have been bestowed upon me. Where do I begin? Is it standing on the subway platform at Hunts Point Avenue setting out for my first gig, or is it twenty-one years later, shaking the hand of President Lyndon Johnson in the East Room of the White House? Kathy has never failed to remind me that, "You have really led an incredible life." It was only on very special occasions, however, that I would stop and take the time to realize, Wow! Mel Torme is singing with the jazz ensemble, or Timofei Dokshizer is here at NIU conducting a clinic with my students and performing with our wind ensemble! In all honesty, much of what was going on during those times was just another day at work. How wonderful it was, how *fortunate* I was, to get up almost every morning of my life and feel excited about what the day would bring. The ordinary was extraordinary.

People began asking me, almost from the first day of my retirement from NIU, "Do you miss it?" My reply was always that I don't miss the faculty meetings, the search committees, and the preparation that was involved in my sixty-to-seventy hour work week. What I did miss was the wonderful rapport I had with my students. Some of them became so close to me that they were, and are, almost like my own children, growing up and leaving the nest.

Having had six children of my own—three sons and three daughters—I know this dynamic well. My oldest, Scott, works as an insurance salesman in Naperville, Illinois. His sister, Lisa Robin, lives in Rome, New York and is working on her degree in drug counseling. My adopted daughter, Lisa Marie, is working toward her degree in graphic design at Colorado State University. My son, Christopher, teaches English as a second language in Tokyo, and daughter Jennifer lives and works in Chicago. Joshua, my youngest, works and writes for "The Onion" as editor-in-chief and general manager of its AV Club. As they scatter and create their own lives, I miss the kind of rapport and interaction we have enjoyed as well.

I cried the day I received a most beautiful and touching letter from a former student, which follows this chapter. It is kept in a special drawer in my desk at home, along with hundreds of other letters that students have been kind enough to send to me over the years, in their efforts to stay in touch.

These are the real rewards after you retire. I never met a teacher who believed they would become wealthy by going into the field of education. What we should realize is that our riches and rewards derive from doing our job well, both giving us satisfaction and often profoundly impacting our students as well. As that special letter shows, there is a kind of ripple effect, and that is what makes us as teachers so proud.

I have been fortunate to hear from so many former students, some of whom I'm lucky enough to see regularly. Three of them, along with their families, recently celebrated with Kathy and me our thirtieth year of meeting each summer for a cookout. It's quite moving to see my former students with their grandchildren. I am also proud that all three of them have contributed to making the world a much better place. Mark Bettcher and Vern Spevak are two of the most inspiring teachers of students of any age that I have ever observed. David Katz has had a distinguished career, not only musically, but in the medical field. To see these men develop over the years into great husbands, fathers, professionals, and remarkable human beings warms my heart.

I retired from NIU in May 1997, hoping to extend my clinics and solo performances all over the country. Until then, they had been limited by the sheer size of my workload. The ten years that followed were some of the happiest in my entire career.

Phil Collins, the international pop star, contacted me, via Quincy Jones in 1997, and asked me to put together a big band for a two-month world tour, an incredible experience that I describe in the chapter "Very Special People." In 2001, I toured in Germany with Craig Roselieb and Brayer Teague, along with the very talented young musicians from Downers Grove Illinois's District 99, first at their sister city Betigheim-Bissengen, and then in other cities all over Germany. We had the distinct pleasure and honor of being adopted by the wonderful Rausch family whose warm welcome immediately made us comforable in their home. This same trip was repeated in 2005.

2006 became a very special year, as it launched my third career into the wonderful world of standup comedy. Since our retirement, Kathy and I have spent all our winters at our home in Bradenton, Florida. On our tenth wedding anniversary, I took Kathy to Lake Tahoe, and we visited our first comedy club there. We enjoyed ourselves so much that we dropped in on McCurdy's Comedy Theater in Sarasota when we got back to Florida.

I met the club's owner, Les McCurdy there one night and proceeded to do what I do: I told Les a joke. He invited me to come and perform on one of their weekly open mic nights—to get up on stage for five minutes, see how I liked it, and see how they liked me. I took him up on this, and after my first five-minute effort, Les asked me to appear on a future show with a ten-minute set.

For the past four years, I have been introduced as the "guest comedian" for the evening, performing a fifteen-to-thirty minute set before the headliner appears. My audiences at McCurdy's have been absolutely wonderful, and the most exhilarating part has been the response from the younger generation. Nothing, of course, is like the feeling you get when the audience reacts to your material, and you realize that, for the short amount of time you have been on stage, you've gotten them to laugh and forget about their troubles.

I couldn't have found a better club in which to start my new career. Les McCurdy is a very special man, with a real gift for communicating with a new audience each night. By the time Les is through talking and laughing with the audience, each succeeding performer knows they can walk out and encounter people who are ready to laugh and enjoy themselves. His kindness, warmth, and great caring for his fellow human beings insures him a very special place in heaven. Les and his beautiful wife Pam for many years have made Sarasota a better place to live.

Whenever I have shared my new standup career with friends or family, the reaction has always been the same: "You'd be perfect at that!" It is, of course, one thing to tell somebody a joke and a very different thing to walk out on stage and tell that joke to two hundred paying customers. I found out there is also a generation gap in humor, one afternoon I told my youngest son Joshua a joke that had always elicited great laughs, but only drew a blank stare from him.

I meet the generational issue head-on by always walking through the comedy club's audience prior to show time, getting a sense of the age of the people there that night. It has been exhilarating for me to connect with audiences who are between twenty-one and forty years old. I feel like my old friend Tony Bennett, when he was rediscovered by the MTV crowd!

It's been part of my act to tell the audience that as funny as jokes may be, nothing beats real-life humor. How about this? At one of my appointments with my cardiologist, the nurse came in to take my weight, blood pressure, and pulse. She sat down with her charts, with her back to me, and asked, "What brings you here today, Mr. Modell?" My immediate reply: "My period is late!" She laughed so hard she left to repeat the line to all the other nurses. Another one of my favorite real-life jokes came in July 1969, when my wife was in her ninth month of pregnancy, a very *large* pregnancy. As we placed our groceries from our cart to the checkout counter at the local supermarket, an older woman touched me on the shoulder to ask, "Is your wife pregnant?" "No," I told her, "She's been this way for three years. We think it's water!" These stories illustrate why the line I always use is, "My mouth never saw a stop sign.

Years ago, my brother Sandy's wife, Esther, made the remark to my wife Kathy that "Ronnie was the daughter mom never had." Though I truly believe that I was blessed with the two best brothers in the world, secretly I had always wanted a sister. I am lucky that two women in my life have taken on that role. First, my dear friend Jean Colford Pinkston, whom I met in 1960 when we were both playing in the Dallas Symphony Orchestra. For fifty-three years, we have shared the true meaning of the word "Friend." I have also enjoyed a forty-year friendship with Sari Max Fiss, an incredibly gifted woman who amazes me with her creativity and boundless energy, always trying to make the world a better place. We are always there for each other, especially in times of strife.

These precious words were sent to me after Sari read the final draft:

There are men who are intellectually inclined, curious about the world and how it works. They go about obtaining answers as thoroughly as possible. There are men who are creative and wear their emotions for the world to see; making an impact on all those they encounter with the sheer force of their earnest desire to touch lives, to inspire.

There are men who pursue excellence in their given field. They give a hundred and ten percent where a combination of superb qualities is mandated by the standard-bearers. And, there are men who reach deep inside to find the common denominator; often humor, that once expressed, will elevate another's being (often relieving some pain along the way). Then, there's Ron Modell. A man I am proud to call "friend" for forty-two years. I watched Ron's extraordinary book, "Loved Being Here with You," unfold and listened to familiar and unfamiliar anecdotes being readied for the page. As he shared an early draft, I realized that Ron is ALL of the above-mentioned men combined; And if that weren't enough: a wonderful son, brother, father, grandfather, great-grandfather, and husband. If his performing, teaching, coaching careers begged for anything, it was that they were well-documented (another career: author!). You are a gift to me. I am so proud of your book and of you, my friend.

My two brothers, Sandy and Lance, and I were also always there for each other. In addition to my unconditional love for them, I had the utmost respect and admiration for their work as teachers. It was perplexing to me that I never could get Sandy to talk about his work in New York City with especially difficult and troubled students. He finally broke his silence one night in 1977 when he visited my home in Sycamore. Dizzy Gillespie joined us for dinner that evening, as he was appearing that week with the NIUjazz ensemble.

After much prodding, Sandy relented and gave us one example of the kind of things he dealt with in his work. Recently he had been assigned the task of retrieving a thirteen-year-old girl from her parents, who had been forcing her into prostitution to feed their heroin habit. Sandy had to go into a neighborhood that was so dangerous that Dizzy immediately commented, "I'm Dizzy Gillespie, and I wouldn't go into that neighborhood even with the police!" What Dizzy didn't know was that the people in the neighborhood knew and trusted Sandy, so much that they had given him the nickname "Maestro," not for any musical ability, but because everyone knew he was there to do good for the kids. Even the local gang members knew him and would not touch his car.

When Sandy took one step into the young girl's building, he quickly saw there were a number of strung-out junkies on the first set of stairs, while behind him across the street two tough-looking guys were approaching. Sandy's incredible street smarts took him to the closest store, where he called the nearest police precinct and reported hearing five gunshots at the apartment building. It only took two or three minutes before five squad cars pulled up. Now Sandy simply walked up the steps, retrieved the girl, and delivered her safely to DCFS (Department of Children and Family Services).

When I think of Lance, which I do every day, I always hear that line "The good die young." Lance had just retired after a brilliant career as a high school math teacher, when he suddenly died of a heart attack. He had served many years as the chairman of the math department at West Hempstead High School on Long Island and had been voted "Teacher of the Year" many, many times. The respect he commanded as a math educator was such that he was asked to be part of the team that wrote the New York State Board of Regents math exam. After his death, Lance was posthumously voted into the New York State Math Hall of Fame.

While my comedy career marked a new beginning, this was inevitably the time of my life when some things had to end. Sometimes these were quick, spontaneous decisions, while other times they were slowly and deliberately thought out. For example, my decision to quit umpiring after twenty-two years, came as a sudden impulse. I started that day like any other day of umpiring, calling a doubleheader at Kishwaukee College. In the third inning, I suddenly asked myself, "What are you doing here?" It was clear at that moment, this was the end. At the end of the half-inning, I walked over to the fence and asked a fellow umpire if he could do the second game for me. I finalized my departure by speaking with manager Al Kooper, asking if he could find a substitute for me for the rest of the season; though of course I would honor my commitment if that proved impossible. I had had no warning that this decision would suddenly come upon me.

It was very different, however, when I made the enormous decision; six-to-nine months beforehand, to retire from ever again playing the trumpet. Here my reasons were clear-cut. Most important was the knowledge that I had played at a certain level of technical and musical virtuosity for most of my career, and I was not willing to go even a fraction below that. It was getting harder: things that had been easy for me on the trumpet now required much more practice time.

I was realistic enough to know that to put in the necessary time effort, and dedication needed to maintain my level of playing was just not going to be in my future. I realized I had accomplished all that I had set out to do in my chosen field, and it was time now to move on.

My very first public appearance in the DeKalb-Sycamore area was on July 4, 1969 with the DeKalb Municipal Band, conducted by the wonderful musician Dee Palmer. Dee was certainly the heart and soul of music in DeKalb County. So it seemed only fitting and right to end my career on the stage where it had begun, with the DeKalb Municipal Band under Dee Palmer's baton. I concluded my last concert on July 4

2007 at the Band's summer venue in beautiful Hopkins Park, with a great arrangement of the Sinatra classic, "My Way." It was a hot July night with the temperature in the mid 90s, and as I removed my black tuxedo jacket in the dressing room afterwards, here came my beautiful wife Kathy, in tears, to hug me tightly and say, "I won't ever get to hear you play again."

What made my decision to give up the trumpet a bit easier was that at the age of sixty-five, I was introduced to the wonderful world of golf. Kathy had come to me with a proposition: if I would learn to play golf (she is an accomplished golfer), then she would learn to play bridge. We have played and enjoyed hundreds of rounds of golf together in the past thirteen years, but we never got around to playing bridge. Kathy did make the attempt, but after taking some lessons and observing some serious bridge players, she decided bridge would not be part of her retirement life. But golf continues to give us great pleasure, and anyone who has ever played the game knows that it's you against a little white ball, and what a challenge that presents every day you step up to the first tee.

A few years ago, playing at one of my favorite courses in Sarasota, Florida, I hit a terrible shot and was about to fling my golf club up in disgust. Suddenly, however, I looked down at the ground and had an epiphany: there were so many people under the ground who would have loved to be up here on a beautiful sunny day playing golf. From that moment on, no matter how badly I played, this thought was with me: I was grateful to be here, and I would always have a chance to hit a better shot.

In March 1994, after my first of four angioplasties, I walked into my first cardio rehab session to read a banner with the words, "Getting Old is Not for Sissies!" My cousin Emil Davidson recently put this into perspective as he commented that most conversations now with friends and family, inevitably turn into an "organ recital." My wish is that by sharing my story with you, it has touched your life in a very special way, and I hope you loved bein' here with me as much as I loved bein' here with you.

Dear Ron,

Being almost fifty years old now, I was recently reflecting on my life, especially my experiences as a trumpet player and music teacher. While I've always been grateful to you for giving me the opportunity to go to college and all the experiences that went with it, I've never taken the time to tell you how much it meant to my life.

I don't know if you remember, but I was not accepted to NIU because of my poor grades in high school. Somehow though you were able to pull some strings and get me in. I've often imagined what would have become of me if it weren't for you doing that. I'd probably be working behind the counter at Best Buy or something. Instead I've traveled all over the world as a musician, enjoyed a career doing something I love, and have become an acceptable teacher myself.

I now have a beautiful wife, Margaret, two wonderful sons, Matthew and Jacob, a nice teaching job, a nice house in the suburbs, and all in all have a pretty good life. That may not have happened it if weren't for you. I can only imagine how many others have similar stories as the ripple effect of your career has to have touched thousands of lives as your students have passed on what they got from you. I will forever be grateful to you and hope I have repaid you, at least in part, through my efforts with my own students over the years.

I thought about calling you to tell you this personally but didn't think I could convey the depth of my gratitude without getting choked up. I hope all is well with you and your family and wish you all the best always.

Sincerely,
Scott Wagstaff

To Ron on the occasion of your retirement:

> *The art of music serves as a force for healing the world and offering people a chance to celebrate in one common language. By teaching this language, you have allowed cultural differences to be forgotten and given people something that no royalty, government, or vast wealth has ever been able to legislate or buy: a way for people to understand one another.*
>
> *Steve Duchrow*
> *Director of Cultural Arts*
> *University Programming and Activities*
> *Northern Illinois University*

GLOSSARY

accidentals

sharps and flats, with sharps raising a note, and flats lowering it

charts

arrangements, either original music, or any piece of published music arranged for any size group

chops

endurance

del segno sign

a sign designating where you should return to

first ending - second ending

when section of music is repeated

forte

loud

freilach

a Jewish dance, lively, happy, most well known freilach "Hava Nagi-lah" gig

a playing engagement

improvisation

the ability to leave the melody, and create new notes each time

Klezmer music

traditional Jewish music

mezzo forte

half as loud

pedal tones

notes below the lowest natural note on the trumpet

pianissimo

very softly

principal player

he leader of their section

scherzo

fast

sight reading

seeing and playing music for the first time

transposition

changing the notes you see to the correct key

unisons

where the section is playing the same notes at the same time

wood shedding

working to perfect a piece

Made in the USA
Lexington, KY
19 August 2014